njoy thi
renew

50 WALKS IN
Hampshire &
the Isle of Wight

50 Walks in Hampshire & the Isle of Wight

Published by AA Publishing (a trading name of AA Media Limited, whose registered office is Fanum House, Basing View, Basingstoke, Hampshire RG21 4EA; registered number 06112600)

First published 2001
Second edition 2009
Third edition 2014
This edition 2019

Field checked and updated by
Richard Marchi

Mapping in this book is derived from the following products:
OS Landranger 174 (walks 2, 3, 5)
OS Landranger 175 (walks1, 4)
OS Landranger 184 (walks 28, 29)
OS Landranger 185 (walks 6, 8,–10, 15–19, 21–24)
OS Landranger 186 (walks 7, 11–14, 20)
OS Landranger 195 (walks 30, 31)
OS Landranger 196 (walks 26, 27, 32, 34, 35, 37–50)
OS Landranger 197 (walks 25, 36)
OS Explorer 22 (walk 33)

© Crown copyright and database rights 2019 Ordnance Survey. 100021153.

ISBN: 978-0-7495-8119-0
ISBN (SS): 978-0-7495-7580-9

A CIP catalogue record for this book is available from the British Library.

Series management: Clare Ashton
Editor: Julia Sandford-Cooke
Designer: Tom Whitlock
Digital imaging & repro: Ian Little
Cartography provided by the Mapping Services Department of AA Publishing.

Printed and bound in Italy by Printer Trento Srl

A05661

We would like to thank the following photographers, companies and picture libraries for their assistance in the preparation of this book. Abbreviations for the picture credits are as follows: AA = World Travel Library, Alamy = Alamy Stock Photo
12/13 Adrian Campbell-Burt/Alamy; 23 Simon Tranter Photography/Alamy; 45 AA/J Tims; 71 Britpix/Alamy; 85 mauritius images GmbH/Alamy; 101 Brian Eyley images/Alamy; 123 DAVID EASTLEY/Alamy; 139 Hilda Weges/Alamy; 149 Steve Hawkins Photography/Alamy; 159 Nikreates/Alamy

AA

50 WALKS IN
Hampshire &
the Isle of Wight

CONTENTS

The walks

WALK		GRADIENT	DISTANCE	
23	Romsey	▲	5.9 miles (9.5km)	86
24	Meon Valley	▲▲	7 miles (11.3km)	89
25	Chalton	▲▲▲	7.8 miles (12.5km)	92
26	Hambledon	▲	6.4 miles (10.25km)	95
27	Wickham	▲	4 miles (6.4km)	98
28	Breamore	▲	5.5 miles (8.9km)	102
29	Rockbourne	▲	5 miles (8.1km)	105
30	Fritham	▲	5.7 miles (9.2km)	108
31	Minstead	▲	5.3 miles (8.6km)	111
32	Lyndhurst	▲	3.4 miles (5.5km)	114
33	New Forest	▲	9.5 miles (15.3km)	117
34	Bursledon	▲	5.9 miles (9.5km)	120
35	Titchfield	▲	7 miles (11.3km)	124
36	Emsworth Harbour	▲	4.8 miles (7.8km)	127
37	Farlington Marshes	▲	2.5 miles (4km)	130
38	Portsmouth	▲	3.5 miles (5.6km)	133
39	Beaulieu	▲	4.8 miles (7.7km)	134
40	Exbury	▲	6.6 miles (10.7km)	136
41	Keyhaven	▲	5.4 miles (8.7km)	140
42	Shalfleet	▲	3.7 miles (5.6km)	146
43	Wootton Bridge	▲▲	3.3 miles (5.3km)	150
44	Bembridge	▲▲	5.8 miles (9.3km)	153
45	Carisbrooke	▲▲	6.5 miles (10.5km)	156
46	Yarmouth	▲	4.1 miles (6.7km)	160
47	Freshwater	▲	6.1 miles (9.8km)	163
48	Brighstone	▲▲	8.6 miles (13.8km)	166
49	Godshill	▲▲	4.6 miles (7.4km)	170
50	Blackgang Chine	▲▲	5.4 miles (8.7km)	173

HOW TO USE THIS BOOK

Each walk starts with an information panel giving all the information you will need about the walk at a glance, including its relative difficulty, distance and total amount of ascent. Difficulty levels and gradients are as follows:

Difficulty of walk

● Easy

● Intermediate

● Hard

Gradient

▲ Some slopes

▲▲ Some steep slopes

▲▲▲ Several very steep slopes

Maps

Every walk has its own route map. We also suggest a relevant AA or Ordnance Survey map to take with you, allowing you to view the area in more detail. The time suggested is the minimum for reasonably fit walkers and doesn't allow for stops.

Route map legend

_ _ ➡ _ _	Walk route	▢	Built-up area
❶	Route waypoint	▢	Woodland area
_ _ _ _	Adjoining path	🚻	Toilet
●	Place of interest	🅿	Car park
⌂	Steep section	▦	Picnic area
⧚	Viewpoint	)(	Bridge

Start points

The start of each walk is given as a six-figure grid reference prefixed by two letters referring to a 100km square of the National Grid. More information on grid references can be found on most OS and AA Walker's Maps.

Dogs

We have tried to give dog owners useful advice about how dog friendly each walk is. Please respect other countryside users. Keep your dog under control, especially around livestock, and obey local bylaws and other dog control notices.

Car parking

Many of the car parks suggested are public, but occasionally you may have to park on the roadside or in a lay-by. Please be considerate about where you leave your car, ensuring that you are not on private property or access roads, and that gates are not blocked and other vehicles can pass safely.

Walks locator map

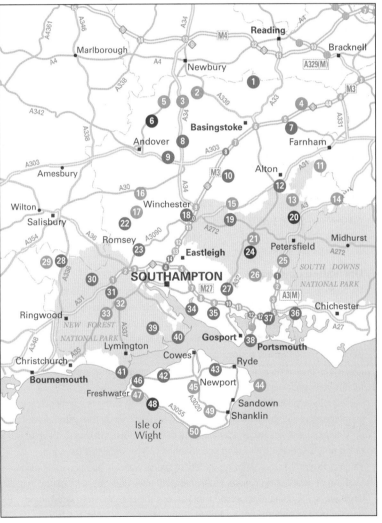

EXPLORING THE AREA

Why should you go walking in Hampshire or the Isle of Wight? Walking is enjoyable exercise; it helps maintain fitness and takes you to places no car ever could. And Hampshire and the Isle of Wight have history in abundance and a diverse and interesting range of landscapes, linked by an enviable network of over 3,000 miles (4,800km) of rights of way.

You can stride out across the high, rolling, chalk downland of the north Hampshire 'highlands' with far-reaching views, walk through steep, beech-clad 'hangers' close to the Sussex border, or meander along peaceful paths through unspoilt river valleys, etched by the sparkling trout streams of the Test, Itchen, Avon and Meon. Alternatively, you can wander across lonely salt marshes and beside fascinating coastal inlets or, perhaps, explore the beautiful medieval forest and heathland of the New Forest, the jewel in Hampshire's crown. You will find that the county's extensive web of footpaths, bridleways and ancient byways crosses them all. There are also eight distinctively waymarked long-distance paths, including the Avon Valley Path in the west, the Hangers Way in the east, the Wayfarers' Walk and Test Way which traverse the county from north to south, and the South Downs Way, which terminates in Winchester, the ancient capital of Wessex and England and Hampshire's county town.

Unrivalled landscape

Hampshire's varied landscape of hills and heaths, downlands and forests, valleys and coast is without rival in southern England. Combine these varied landscapes and terrains with secluded and idyllic villages, complete with thatched and timber-framed cottages and Norman churches, elegant Georgian market towns, historic ports and cities, restored canals and ancient abbeys, forts and castles, and you have a county that is paradise for the walking fraternity.

Equally appealing, and a short ferry voyage away, is the Isle of Wight, an enchanting island with magnificent coastal views, sandy bays, sheltered creeks, picturesque villages and a unique blend of old-world charm. Despite being only 23 miles (37km) long and 13 miles (21km) wide, this diamond-shaped haven offers an amazing variety of scenery and, in addition to 64 miles (103km) of exhilarating coastal paths, has 500 miles (805km) of footpaths and bridleways, including eight inland trails across the island's breezy downland and unspoilt farmland. For two weeks during May and October, the Isle of Wight Walking Festival draws on the island's special appeal. Among the guided and unguided walks offered are fun walks for families and challenging hikes for enthusiasts.

The walks in this book are circular and vary in length from 1.9 miles (3km) to 9.5 miles (15.3km). Most are rural, except for a stroll around the historic dockland in Old Portsmouth and a city walk that incorporates the celebrated sights and narrow streets of Winchester. Several walks start and end in towns, such as New Alresford, Romsey and Stockbridge, but meander into the surrounding countryside. All have been devised with the recreational rambler in mind, so you don't need to be a serious hiker to undertake them.

PUBLIC TRANSPORT

Either the start points of the walks, or the villages en route, are within easy reach from public transport. Several start close to railway stations.For train times call the 24-hour National Rail Enquiries line on 03457 48 49 50.

For information on ferry travel to the Isle of Wight see wightlink.co.uk (Portsmouth–Fishbourne or Ryde, Lymington–Yarmouth) or redfunnel. co.uk (Southampton–East or West Cowes).

You can also get information about local public transport links on travelinesw.com.

WALKING IN SAFETY

All these walks are suitable for any reasonably fit person, but less experienced walkers should try the easier walks first. Route-finding is usually straightforward, but you will find that an Ordnance Survey or AA walking map is a useful addition to the route maps and descriptions; recommendations can be found in the information panels.

Risks

Although each walk here has been researched with a view to minimising the risks to the walkers who follow its route, no walk in the countryside can be considered to be completely free from risk. Walking in the outdoors will always require a degree of common sense and judgement to ensure that it is as safe as possible.

- Be particularly careful on cliff paths and in upland terrain, where the consequences of a slip can be very serious.

- Remember to check tidal conditions before walking on the seashore.

- Some sections of route are by, or cross, busy roads. Take care, and remember that traffic is a danger even on minor country lanes.

- Be careful around farmyard machinery and livestock, especially if you have children with you.

- Be aware of the consequences of changes in the weather, and check the forecast before you set out. Carry spare clothing and a torch if you are walking in the winter months. Remember that the weather can change very quickly at any time of the year, and in moorland and heathland areas, mist and fog can make route-finding much harder. Don't set out in these conditions unless you are confident of your navigation skills in poor visibility.

- In summer remember to take account of the heat and sun; wear a hat and carry water.

- On walks away from centres of population you should carry a whistle and survival bag. If you do have an accident that means you require help from the emergency services, make a note of your position as accurately as possible and dial 999.

Countryside Code
Respect other people:

- Consider the local community and other people enjoying the outdoors.

- Co-operate with people at work in the countryside. For example, keep out of the way when farm animals are being gathered or moved, and follow directions from the farmer.

- Don't block gateways, driveways or other paths with your vehicle.
- Leave gates and property as you find them, and follow paths unless wider access is available, such as on open country or registered common land (known as 'open access land').
- Leave machinery and farm animals alone – don't interfere with animals, even if you think they're in distress. Try to alert the farmer instead.
- Use gates, stiles or gaps in field boundaries if you can – climbing over walls, hedges and fences can damage them and increase the risk of farm animals escaping.
- Our heritage matters to all of us – be careful not to disturb ruins and historic sites.

Protect the natural environment:
- Take your litter home. Litter and leftover food don't just spoil the beauty of the countryside; they can be dangerous to wildlife and farm animals. Dropping litter and dumping rubbish are criminal offences.
- Leave no trace of your visit, and take special care not to damage, destroy or remove features such as rocks, plants and trees.
- Keep dogs under effective control, making sure they are not a danger or nuisance to farm animals, horses, wildlife or other people.
- If cattle or horses chase you and your dog, it is safer to let your dog off the lead – don't risk getting hurt by trying to protect it. Your dog will be much safer if you let it run away from a farm animal in these circumstances, and so will you.
- Everyone knows how unpleasant dog mess is and it can cause infections, so always clean up after your dog and get rid of the mess responsibly – bag it and bin it.
- Fires can be as devastating to wildlife and habitats as they are to people and property – so be careful with naked flames and cigarettes at any time of the year.

Enjoy the outdoors:
- Plan ahead and be prepared for natural hazards, changes in weather and other events.
- Wild animals, farm animals and horses can behave unpredictably if you get too close, especially if they're with their young – so give them plenty of space.
- Follow advice and local signs.

For more information visit naturalengland.org.uk/ourwork/enjoying/countrysidecode

ROMAN CALLEVA AT SILCHESTER

DISTANCE/TIME	4.3 miles (7km) / 2hrs 15min
ASCENT/GRADIENT	302ft (92m) / ▲
PATHS	Field paths and woodland tracks, some stiles
LANDSCAPE	Open farmland, mixed woodland
SUGGESTED MAP	OS Explorer 159 Reading, Wokingham & Pangbourne
START/FINISH	Grid reference: SU643623
DOG FRIENDLINESS	Lead required on Englefield Estate; may need to be lifted over stiles beyond Mortimer
PARKING	Church of St Mary the Virgin, Silchester. Please avoid Sunday mornings, when you should use alternative parking by Point 3
PUBLIC TOILETS	None on route

Tucked between Basingstoke and Reading is a pocket of gently undulating countryside. Here you will find stretches of ancient woodland, open farmland and a web of narrow, leafy lanes leading to isolated farms, secluded villages, stately houses and the site of the Roman town of Calleva Atrebatum.

Calleva was already the prosperous tribal capital of the Atrebates and an administrative centre for a large area before the Romans developed the site following the invasion in AD 43. It became a key military and commercial centre, and important roads radiated from it. Earth ramparts were built to protect the buildings between AD 160 and 200, and the facing walls which you see today were added between AD 250 and 275. The wall, 1.25 miles (2km) round, enclosed broad streets laid out at right angles. The walk begins by the impressive defensive walls, and you should allow time to pause at the information boards dotted around the Town Trail. These offer more detail on the town's development and explain how the encircling walls were built.

Digging up history

The site was thoroughly excavated during Victorian times, exposing a partial plan, including a road network, foundations of buildings and perhaps the earliest-known Christian church in Britain. More recent excavations revealed that Calleva was probably occupied until the 6th or 7th centuries and did not decline in the 5th century, as previously thought. Today, you can see little of the town above ground as the buildings were reburied to protect them from the weather, vegetation, vandals and souvenir hunters. However, excavations continue, with tents in summertime usually marking the latest explorations.

Just off the route is the recently excavated Roman amphitheatre. Built in the 1st century AD on an impressive scale, it could accommodate more than 4,000 spectators on wooden seats above the walls. Here, the citizens came to watch sports, gladiatorial contests and public executions.

Having strolled around the Roman walls, you have another change of scene by walking into Benyon's Inclosure, peaceful mixed woodlands that were once part of Pamber Forest, an ancient forest where King John is reputed to have hunted deer.

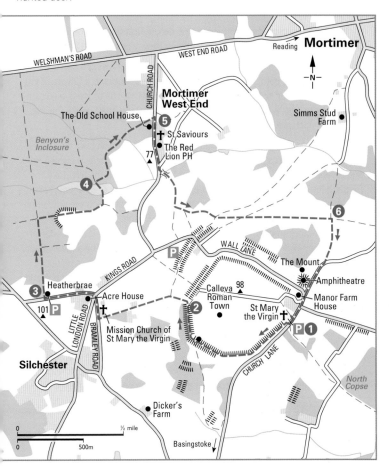

1. From the church, turn right along the road. Just after the bend bear right at a gap, up steps, to follow the Town Trail along the undulating grassy top of the Roman town's perimeter wall. At the South Gate (one of seven such entry points, although only four now remain) go through to the outside of the wall and follow the grassy path, with the wall now on your right. Continue ahead into woodland and follow the clear track round, with the wall looming to the right, to reach a wooden kissing gate at a junction of paths.

2. Turn left along the track through a second, right-hand gate signed to Silchester village. Follow the enclosed footpath to its end and straight ahead onto a gravel lane between houses. Continue ahead to meet the road. Here, turn right, passing the wooden Mission Church of St Mary the Virgin, to reach a road junction. Bear right then immediately turn left at the grassy triangle, which is signed towards Tadley. Walk with care along the road to a cottage

15

called Heatherbrae and a parking area (which could mark the start of the walk on Sunday mornings when parking outside Silchester church is limited).

3. Turn right down the broad gravel track, walking past the gate into the managed woodland of Benyon's Inclosure. Keep straight on this track, until the tracks cross by a green Englefield Estate sign just before the track starts to descend. Turn right here, following the path, at first flat and then gradually downhill to a fork. Keep left and cross the causeway beside the lake.

4. Where the main path curves left, keep right uphill, following a narrow, winding woodland path. Keep ahead across a wide grassy track (25yds (20m) from a gate on your right), and descend into thicker woods to cross a stream via a plank bridge. Keep right at a junction of paths and head uphill. Pass a barrier to reach the road by The Old School House.

5. Turn right, passing the church and The Red Lion pub, then take the second track on the left. Cross a bridge and follow the byway uphill. As it curves right and levels out, look for the yellow waymarker on a post on the left. Take the footpath left through the edge of a copse to a stile and proceed ahead, keeping left along the field edge to a stile. Cross a farm track and climb the stile opposite, then keep to the left-hand edge to a stile in the field corner, before crossing another track and stile. Continue ahead along the left-hand edge of the field, then bear diagonally right across the field to a stile by a gate, about halfway down. Walk diagonally across the next field to a stile by a water trough. Proceed straight ahead towards the power lines to cross a stile beside an oak tree. Bear right round the field edge and pass under power cables to reach a crossroads of tracks.

6. Turn right over a stile, and continue downhill to a plank bridge and a gate. Gently ascend the field and leave via a kissing gate and onto a sunken track. Turn right and pass a thatched cottage (The Mount) on your right. Where the drive meets the lane, a gate on the right leads to the Roman amphitheatre. Walk ahead along Church Lane, keeping right to return to the car park.

Where to eat and drink
The Red Lion, a 16th-century pub, serves pub grub, Sunday roasts and a fine Italian menu, alongside a range of wines and real ales.

What to see
A visit to the Church of St Mary the Virgin, dating from 1180, features Roman bricks incorporated into its walls and buttresses, as well as simple, 13th-century wall-paintings and an organ from about 1860.

While you're there
Visit Reading Museum to see the Silchester Collection, a wealth of items from the Roman town. Most were found during excavations of the area between 1890 and 1909.

EXPLORING ECCHINSWELL

DISTANCE/TIME	2.5 miles (4.1km) / 1hr 15min
ASCENT/GRADIENT	266ft (81m) / ▲ ▲
PATHS	Country tracks, field and woodland paths (may be muddy), some stiles
LANDSCAPE	Wooded farmland with downland views
SUGGESTED MAP	OS Explorer 144 Basingstoke, Alton & Whitchurch
START/FINISH	Grid reference: SU500597
DOG FRIENDLINESS	On lead near grazing livestock and in the woods before Nuthanger Farm
PARKING	Village hall car park, opposite the war memorial
PUBLIC TOILETS	None on route

The rolling chalk hills around Ecchinswell leapt to fame in 1972 as the backdrop for Richard Adams' first novel *Watership Down*. The book became the best-selling Penguin novel of all time and was the inspiration for Art Garfunkel's British number-one hit 'Bright Eyes', from the 1978 film version.

Rabbits' tales

Adams' narrative traces the fortunes of a small band of rabbits who set out into the unknown after one of their number, the clairvoyant Fiver, foresees the destruction of their warren at Sandleford. Leaving many of their fellows behind, the group unites under the gentle leadership of Fiver's brother Hazel and embarks on an epic journey to find a new home.

After setting up home near the northeast corner of the beech hanger on the lofty heights of Watership Down, Hazel realises that his new warren of buck rabbits has no future without females. Helped by Kehaar the seagull, the rabbits relocate to an overcrowded warren at Efrafa and the second half of the book recounts their epic struggle to liberate some of the does from the warren's tyrannical ruler General Woundwort. Meanwhile, Hazel leads a daring raid on nearby Nuthanger Farm, where an earlier sortie had discovered four rabbits — two bucks and two does — living in captivity. The caged rabbits are eventually rescued from their hutch and return to the warren at Watership Down; but, in the confusion, Hazel suffers a gunshot wound.

In the early stages of the walk, you'll meander beside a tiny brook before striking out across farmland that would be familiar to the heroes of Adams' novel. Then, you'll climb beside woodlands for open views over the valley towards Watership Down and the narrow beech hanger where the rabbits established their warren. This is the countryside that Hazel's raiding party cross on their way to the next landmark, Nuthanger Farm. Beneath its tall chimneys and clay-tile roof, this charming building is likely to have changed little since Adams first described it in his novel more than 40 years ago.

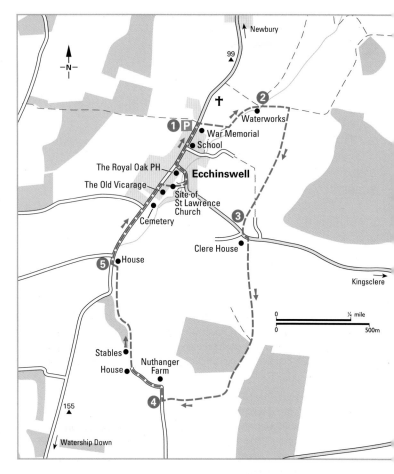

1. Leave the car park by the vehicle entrance, cross the road and take the footpath beside the war memorial. After a few paces, bear left onto a narrow woodland path, cross a plank bridge and continue past a turning on your right with two bridges to the T-junction by a small waterworks building.

2. Turn right, cross the stream and continue for 150yds (137m) before turning off onto the waymarked path across the open field on your right. Continue through a gap in the opposite hedge and over a plank bridge, then follow the winding hedge on your right to the plank bridge and stile in the far corner of the field. (Ignore an earlier path to the right). Climb the stile and cross the next field to the top corner to reach the road at a stile by a gate.

3. Turn left along the road for 60yds (55m), pass the entrance to Clere House and turn right onto the signposted footpath. Keep ahead between fields and then along the top of a wooded bank. Keep left where a track joins from the right, then follow the path around the copse on your right and continue along the enclosed path. Bear right as the path matures into a grassy farm track with views ahead to the left of Watership Down.

4. Turn right onto the gravel lane at the T-junction, swing left in front of Nuthanger Farm and follow the winding drive as it bends down to the right by a house to a wooden stable building. Take a right here onto the narrow path, which continues as a sunken way with open views towards Ecchinswell on your right. The path widens as it drops into the valley to meet the village lane by a newly built part-timber-clad, part-flint red-tiled property.

5. Bear right along the lane, passing the small graveyard on your right. Just beyond the adjacent Old Vicarage, turn right along the path through the grassy site of the old church of St Lawrence. Cross the footbridge and turn left along the road crossing over the stream to the junction by The Royal Oak; turn right here and walk past the school to the car park.

Where to eat and drink

Local ales and home-cooked meals await you in the cosy bar of The Royal Oak, which also has a smart restaurant. Behind the pub, the riverside garden is the venue for summer barbecues, as well as al fresco cocktails served from the thatched rum shack. Dogs are welcome on their leads.

What to see

As you pass the site of the old St Lawrence church, look out for the gravestone of former churchwarden John Digweed, who was the only person to have been buried here. Together with his relatives at Steventon, John Digweed was a friend of Jane Austen and her family. The dilapidated old church was demolished in 1854 and replaced by the present building a couple of years later.

While you're there

Just a couple of miles to the west, Sandham Memorial Chapel is surely one of the National Trust's most unusual properties (open Wednesday to Sunday in the summer, weekends only rest of year). The interior of this modest red-brick building is covered with dramatic paintings by Stanley Spencer (1891–1959), a medical orderly and soldier during World War I. You're welcome to picnic among the fruit trees in the garden.

HIGH ABOVE HIGHCLERE CASTLE

DISTANCE/TIME	8.4 miles (13.5km) / 4hrs 15min
ASCENT/GRADIENT	1007ft (307m) / ▲ ▲
PATHS	Tracks, field and woodland paths, some roads, 6 stiles
LANDSCAPE	Open downland and farmland, with patches of woodland
SUGGESTED MAP	OS Explorer 144 Basingstoke, Alton & Whitchurch
START/FINISH	Grid reference: SU463576
DOG FRIENDLINESS	Keep on lead on Beacon Hill March–July and around livestock
PARKING	Beacon Hill car park off A34
PUBLIC TOILETS	None on route

Due to the steep gradient leading to the summit of Beacon Hill, the highest point of the North Hampshire Downs at 857ft (261m), it's advisable to climb the hill at the start of the walk. Don't miss the Earl of Carnarvon's grave and the views across the Highclere Estate to Highclere Castle (open July–August).

Set within a landscape of parkland and wooded hills designed by 'Capability' Brown between 1774 and 1777, Highclere Castle is a magnificent pastiche of a medieval castle, impressively grand inside and out. But Hampshire's largest mansion is actually early Victorian, designed and built in neo-Elizabethan style by Charles Barry, architect of the Houses of Parliament, between 1839 and 1842 around an earlier house. It is the home of the Earls of Carnarvon and the sumptuous interior, particularly the great hall, the library, the Rococo-style drawing room and the dining room, are adorned with fine portraits of the Earl's family, the Herberts.

Of the seven Earls of Carnarvon that have resided at Highclere, it is the 5th that we are interested in. George Herbert had been fascinated by Egypt and archaeology from an early age and, after a serious accident in 1902, he spent time recuperating there. From 1906 he began sponsoring archaeological investigations, employing Howard Clark, an expert Egyptologist. In 1922, after years of excavating in the Valley of Kings near Thebes, they discovered the tomb of Tutankhamun and treasures that had been buried for over 3,000 years. The 5th Earl died a year later from an infected mosquito bite, which led to the stories of the curse of Tutankhamun. His body was returned to England and, as instructed, he was buried at the top of Beacon Hill overlooking his beloved estate. Much of his collection was sold after his death, but some artefacts were discovered in a hiding place in the castle in 1987. You can see these on display as you tour the mansion. Unfortunately, outside July and August, you will have to be content with viewing the castle and grounds from the 5th Earl's grave on Beacon Hill or on television as the sumptuous location for Downton Abbey.

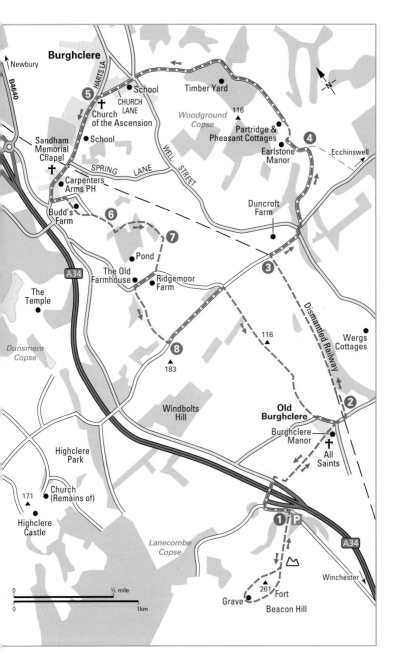

1. Climb Beacon Hill at the start or end of the walk. Leave the car park via the access road and cross the A34 bridge to reach a T-junction. Take the footpath opposite, downhill to a gate and walk along the field's edge to Old Burghclere. Pass beside the churchyard wall and Burghclere Manor. Continue down the drive and go through a gate onto a lane and then proceed ahead, crossing the

old railway bridge and taking the path left to enter a field via a kissing gate.

2. Keep to the left-hand field edge, leaving through a kissing gate and enter woodland. After a few steps, bear left onto the old trackbed. Turn right and follow the track and later a narrow path for half a mile (800m) to a bridge.

3. Bear left up a chalky path just before the bridge and turn right over the bridge. Gently descend to a lane, turn left and then right, signed 'Ecchinswell'. After 50yds (46m), take the waymarked bridleway left. Keep to this tree-lined path to a gravel drive and turn left.

4. At the imposing gates, go through the side gate and follow the track through the grounds of Earlstone Manor, passing ponds, and exit through a gate, then pass a pair of cottages. Proceed through or close to woodland for a mile (1.6km) to a road. Keep ahead along Church Lane in Burghclere, signed to Sandham Memorial Chapel, passing the primary school on your left.

5. Turn left by the church and keep to the road, crossing over the former railway line and continuing past the Memorial Chapel and the Carpenters Arms, before turning left along a metalled dead-end lane. Pass Ashold Farm, then take the footpath right before the road bends between gardens to a stile. Skirt round Budd's Farm across three fields via three more stiles and then go right on the path through trees to a stile.

6. Turn right along the field edge, following it left in the corner. Drop down to a fingerpost and turn right along a boardwalk into woodland. At a broken stile, turn right along the woodland edge, then right again over a plank bridge to a gate.

7. Keep ahead across the pasture towards Ridgemoor Farm. Pass a pond to a gate and track. Turn right, then where it bears right, turn left up a wooded sunken path which rises steadily to reach a track.

8. Turn left to a crossroads and turn right. Head uphill and keep to the undulating track for 0.5 miles (800m) to Old Burghclere. Turn left along the lane and then right along the drive to Burghclere Manor. Retrace your outward steps back to the Beacon Hill car park.

Where to eat and drink

In Burghclere, at the halfway point, is the Carpenters Arms, a homely pub offering food six days a week, an open fire in the winter and a sunny rear terrace with rural views. Highclere Castle has a tearoom for visitors.

What to see

Climb the steep grassy slopes of Beacon Hill to view the Iron Age hill fort close to its highest point. The well-preserved single rampart and ditch enclose the site of around 20 huts. Just inside the defences is the grave of the 5th Earl of Carnarvon, who died in 1923.

While you're there

Visit the Sandham Memorial Chapel (cared for by the National Trust and open Wednesday, Friday and Saturday from March to October) in Burghclere. Built in the 1920s, the interior walls were covered with magnificent paintings by Stanley Spencer between 1926 and 1932. They depict the everyday routine of a soldier's life during the Great War.

HARTLEY WINTNEY AND ELVETHAM

DISTANCE/TIME	4 miles (6.5km) / 2hr 15min
ASCENT/GRADIENT	187ft (57m) / ▲ ▲
PATHS	Field paths, minor roads and woodland tracks, 4 stiles
LANDSCAPE	Golf course, wooded farmland and heath
SUGGESTED MAP	OS Explorer 144 Basingstoke, Alton & Whitchurch
START/FINISH	Grid reference: SU766569
DOG FRIENDLINESS	Can run free on Hazeley Heath, but not during ground bird nesting season
PARKING	Pay-and-display car park off Monachus Lane
PUBLIC TOILETS	At the start

Today, golf is a relatively genteel pastime but, as you walk out across Hartley Wintney golf course, spare a thought for those who came here before you. For this was the site of the early 19th-century workhouse that served Hartley Wintney and a dozen of the surrounding parishes. Opened in the spring of 1835, the building was enlarged the following year and stood here until a new workhouse was constructed at nearby Winchfield in 1871.

Yet just half a mile (800m) from the grinding poverty of the old workhouse stands a building of a different order. From the 15th century, Elvetham Hall was home to the family of Jane Seymour, the third wife of Henry VIII. Henry visited the house at least twice in the 1530s and, in 1591, Edward Seymour, Earl of Hertford, entertained Queen Elizabeth I here. Her entourage stayed in specially built pavilions close to the house and the queen planted an oak tree to commemorate her visit.

After Edward died, his grandson William Seymour, the Marquis of Hertford and Duke of Somerset, inherited the Elvetham Estate. William sold the house in 1649 and, after a complex series of marriages, the property passed into the hands of the Gough-Calthorpe family. The great building stood for another two centuries until it was destroyed by a fire in 1840.

A Victorian phoenix

Enter Frederick Gough, the 4th Baron Calthorpe. He commissioned Samuel Teulon to design the magnificent Victorian Gothic mansion and stables block that rose from the ashes of the old house in 1860. Teulon's building is now home to the sumptuous Elvetham Hotel and you'll have glimpses of the mansion's spectacular roofline soon after leaving the golf course. The hotel stands in 35 acres (14ha) of grounds, with formal gardens, croquet lawn and a broad yew-tree walk. It's said to have the largest magnolia *soulangiana* in England, and Queen Elizabeth's oak tree, which is now over 32 feet (9.8m) in circumference, still stands in the hotel grounds.

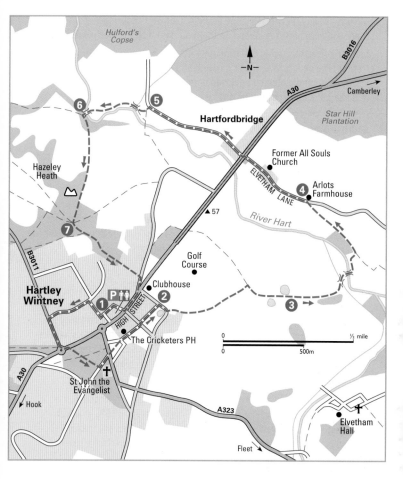

1. Leave the car park by the vehicle exit, walk up Walpole Gardens and turn left along Hartford Road. Turn left at the T-junction, cross the A30, then turn left and right onto the narrow surfaced path to the church of St John the Evangelist. Turn left, cross the A323 at the lights and walk across the green past The Cricketers pub and keep straight on.

2. Turn right up Park Corner Road passing the pond on your right, then turn left over a squeeze stile and turn right onto the signposted path around the edge of golf course. Pass the 2nd tee and follow the fairway until reaching a cross tracks of paths, turn right, signed to Elvetham. Walk past the 3rd tee and veer right after a small pond onto a gravel path. Pass a reed-fringed pond and the 7th tee on your left and keep ahead over the stile out of the golf course.

3. Walk along the right-hand edge of the field, then go through the gap in the far corner and continue to cross over the footbridge, fronted by a kissing gate, and then along the enclosed path between the stream and a fence to a stile. Turn left along the green lane to a kissing gate and keep ahead across the open field towards the red tiled roof of Arlots Farmhouse, and leave the field via a stile beside the right-hand gate in the far hedge.

4. Turn left along Elvetham Lane to the A30 at Hartfordbridge. Cross the main road with care and keep ahead up the road until it bends sharply to the right.

5. Keep ahead through the kissing gate and follow the waymarked route through the paddocks to a pair of gates and a plank bridge. Continue through a kissing gate and along the enclosed path, then go through another kissing gate and keep ahead across the grassy clearing to reach a footbridge that crosses over the River Hart.

6. Cross over, turn left and follow the woodland path over a bridge. Walk alongside the river then bear right up the slope to a junction of paths under overhead power lines, turn left and cross three more plank bridges and walk alongside a stream. Cross two further bridges before climbing to a summit and a firm, wide track.

7. Turn left and, ignoring all turnings, keep left and drop down through the trees to a kissing gate. Keep ahead past the houses onto the narrow path that eventually leads out onto Hunts Common, opposite Hartley Wintney Golf Club. Turn right into the High Street, then right again to the car park.

Where to eat and drink
Standing opposite the cricket field near the start of your walk, The Cricketers offers a good choice of wines and real ales to accompany a menu that suits all tastes, from pan-fried seabass to pub classics, steaks and burgers. Alternatively, try Baristas Coffee House and Bistro in the High Street for breakfast, light lunches and cream teas.

What to see
The walk passes the charming white-painted, weatherboarded former church of All Souls in Hartfordbridge. This was built in 1876 at a cost of just £250 to serve the local Elvetham Estate, and fell eventually into disuse. After more than 25 years of neglect, it was saved from dereliction and restored as a family home.

While you're there
Just a mile (1.6km) from Hartley Wintney, West Green House gardens are a blend of formal box hedges and borders, as well as lakes and follies. They were laid out by Marylyn Abbott, after she leased the gardens from the National Trust in 1993. The gardens are open from early March to late October, but closed on Mondays and Tuesdays.

DOWNLANDS AROUND ASHMANSWORTH

DISTANCE/TIME	5.8 miles (9.4km) / 3hrs 15min
ASCENT/GRADIENT	732ft (223m) / ▲ ▲ ▲
PATHS	Ridge tracks, field paths and country road, 2 stiles
LANDSCAPE	Chalk downland, hidden combes and rolling farmland
SUGGESTED MAP	OS Explorer 131 Romsey, Andover & Test Valley
START/FINISH	Grid reference: SU416575
DOG FRIENDLINESS	Let them off lead along ridge-top track
PARKING	Along village street near war memorial
PUBLIC TOILETS	None on route

The far northwest corner of Hampshire is dominated by a stretch of high chalk downland tumbling across the Berkshire border close to Walbury Hill, the highest chalk hill in England at 947ft (288m). Commonly known as the North Hampshire Downs, this is a remote and peaceful area, with an impressive chalk ridge that affords a magnificent panorama north across Newbury and Berkshire, and west into Wiltshire. South of this lofty escarpment lie rolling hills dotted with ancient woodland, hidden combes and seemingly unchanging isolated communities.

Hill country

Venture west away from the busy A34 and A343 and you'll find yourself on lonely single-track roads, heading through undisturbed hill country, with glorious views unfolding to villages such as Faccombe, Combe, Linkenholt and Vernham Dean. The area must be one of the few areas in the county where you can pause and enjoy the peace and quiet that surrounds you without being rudely interrupted by the intrusive roar of car engines. Sheep dot the pastures, and in high summer the cotton reels of hay, fresh from harvesting, line the fields, and the mewing of buzzards fills the air.

Highest point

You begin your walk in the long, straggling village of Ashmansworth, which at 770ft (235m) is the highest medieval village on chalk anywhere in England. There's a well-spaced mix of farmhouses and cottages built of typical Hampshire flint, brick, timber and thatch. Take a stroll down to the totally unspoilt 12th-century church to view medieval wall paintings and the memorial to the composer Gerald Finzi before setting off for Pilot Hill. Reached via an ancient ridge track, formerly a sheep-droving route, Pilot Hill is, at 937ft (286m), the highest point in Hampshire. As you leave the Wayfarer's Walk, pause to absorb the view across the Berkshire Vale into Oxfordshire. Just a few paces further on, you'll find the view south, across the heart of Hampshire, equally impressive.

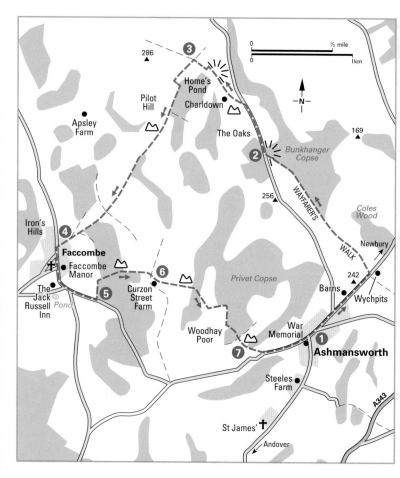

1. Walk north along the village street, keeping ahead at the fork, signed to 'Newbury & Highclere'. In 0.25 miles (400m), just before you reach a house (Wychpits), turn left along a byway (Wayfarer's Walk or WW). Keep to this ancient track along the ridge and beside Bunkhanger Copse to a lane.

2. Turn right and savour the far-reaching views north. In 0.25 miles (400m), bear off left with a WW marker and signed to Charldown, as the lane begins to descend. Follow the stony track along the ridge, passing Charldown and over a low gate, bearing left then right to walk along a field to a crossing of paths.

3. Turn left and head straight across the field (this is Pilot Hill) to a stile beside a large oak. Bear left along the field edge, crossing another stile, then turn right onto a stony track alongside woodland. Steeply descend into a combe, keep ahead at a crossing of tracks and gradually climb, the track eventually merging with a metalled lane.

4. Bear left into Faccombe and turn left along the village street. Pass the church on your right, and keep the wall of Faccombe Manor on your left. Then turn left (signed 'Ashmansworth') by the side of the Manor. In 200yds (183m), take the arrowed path left beside double gates.

5. Keep to the left-hand field edge, following the track right, and steeply descend through woodland. At a junction of tracks, on the edge of a field, bear right to pass two brick-and-flint buildings (Curzon Street Farm).

6. Proceed straight ahead at the crossing of tracks and keep to the main track as it steeply ascends the valley side into woodland. On entering the woodland bear right on wide track, emerge from the trees and keep on the track beside Privet Copse. Where the track forks, take the right fork across the field to join a narrow path straight ahead (as marked by a yellow arrow on a post) through a copse.

7. Drop down onto a track, bear left then immediately right and steeply climb to a gap beside a gate. Then turn left along the road, following it uphill back into Ashmansworth.

Where to eat and drink
Once you've finished the walk, travel the short distance from Ashmansworth north to Hollington Cross and The Yew Tree gastropub. It's on the junction with the A343.

What to see
Faccombe, the most northerly village in the county, is a classic example of an unspoilt estate village. Centred around a large Georgian manor house, it boasts a typical village pond, attractive brick-built cottages and a welcoming village inn, also estate-owned. Named after the Saxon chieftain Facca, the village was once known as Faccombe Upstreet to distinguish it from Faccombe Netherton, now simply Netherton, a mile (1.6km) to the west.

While you're there
Visit the beautiful, unrestored church of St James in Ashmansworth. Look for the 14th-century wall-paintings and for the grave of Gerald Finzi, the composer, who lived in the village from 1939 until his death in 1956. He was best known for his music set to poetry and his place in English music is honoured here in the memorial window in the porch, engraved by Laurence Whistler.

A LOOP FROM HURSTBOURNE TARRANT

DISTANCE/TIME	3.25 miles (5.25km) / 1hr 30min
ASCENT/GRADIENT	381ft (116m) / ▲ ▲
PATHS	Field and woodland paths (some overgrown or muddy sections), 3 stiles
LANDSCAPE	Farmed valley with woodland on the upper slopes
SUGGESTED MAP	OS Explorer 131 Romsey, Andover & Test Valley
START/FINISH	Grid reference: SU385528
DOG FRIENDLINESS	Lead required through paddocks near the start
PARKING	Parish car park, up the lane opposite the church
PUBLIC TOILETS	None on route

The political campaigner William Cobbett wrote chapters of his classic *Rural Rides* in the early years of the 19th century while staying with his friend Joseph Blount at Rookery House on Hurstbourne Hill. In his book he referred to the village many times by its contemporary name of Uphusband.

Crime and punishment

The two friends had much in common and both served prison sentences for their radical views. In spite of this, they continued to champion the rights of ordinary working people.

Blount was known for serving pork and potatoes to poor travellers from a wayfarers' table set up in front of his house and would lend his horse Tinker to help wagons up the long slopes of Hurstbourne Hill. Meanwhile, Cobbett began promoting his radical views in his newspaper, the *Political Register*. After an interlude in the US, Cobbett returned to England in the aftermath of the Peterloo Massacre of 1819. He spoke out against the use of armed force to break up the political demonstration and stood, unsuccessfully, for Parliament in the following year. He then embarked on the project for which he is perhaps best remembered today, riding though southeast England and the Midlands to see the hardships endured by the rural poor.

Cobbett serialised his experiences in his own *Political Register*, before publishing the two volumes of *Rural Rides* in 1830. He still aspired to a Parliamentary seat as the most effective way of improving the lives of ordinary people. After further electoral defeats, he was finally returned as MP for Oldham after the landmark Reform Act of 1832. At Westminster, Cobbett was an advocate of the Poor Law, which was passed a year before he died in 1835.

A short diversion from the centre of the village will take you to Blount's home at Rookery House. It's not open to the public but at the start of your walk you can seek out his grave in St Peter's churchyard. Then, as you descend from Doles Wood on the slopes of Hurstbourne Hill, you'll see the view that William Cobbett believed was one of the finest in southern England.

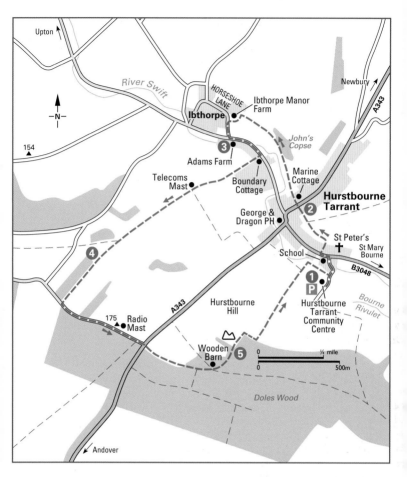

1. From the car park, go back to the B3048 and walk left past the school for 100yds (91m). Cross over, turn right through the kissing gate beside Parsonage Farm, immediately after the large L-shaped thatched barn, and bear left up the slope through a grassy paddock. Bear left through the kissing gate near the top and follow the enclosed path to the A343 near the village shop.

2. Cross the road and follow the path beside Marine Cottage, going through a series of four gates as you cross the paddocks, passing John's Copse on the fenced path towards a large thatched barn. Just before the barn, turn left through the gate and follow the track. Go through a gate beside Ibthorpe Manor Farm to meet Horseshoe Lane, turning left to the village road.

3. Cross and turn left. Pass the former Methodist chapel and turn right up the track immediately before Boundary Cottage. Climb steadily to the stile that marks a fork in the path near the top. Keep ahead over the second (left-hand) stile, into a field, and briefly follow the left-hand hedge before crossing the field towards the left of the house.

4. Climb over the stile and follow the somewhat overgrown path to a road, then turn left to reach a junction with the A343. Cross the main road and keep

ahead along the edge of Doles Wood, ignoring the track on your right just after the woods close in on your left. Then, 100yds (91m) further on, turn left at the waymarker post and bear right along a woodland path that drops to the corner of a wire fence.

5. Follow the waymarked route steeply downhill beside the fence to reach a field. Turn right for 100yds (91m) along the woodland edge, then turn left and drop down towards the village. At the foot of the hill, go through the gate into the recreation ground and turn right to the car park.

Where to eat and drink

The George and Dragon in the village has recently been renovated and serves breakfast, lunch and dinner, local ales and a range of wines, and has rooms available for those wishing to stay overnight in the area. Additionally there are two pubs in nearby St Mary Bourne, The George and Bourne Valley Inn.

What to see

As you approach the church from the lychgate, you'll see Joseph Blount's grave on the left, at the foot of an ancient yew tree. Blount wanted his gravestone to be large and flat enough for children to play marbles on it. Families, please note!

While you're there

Life-size models and dioramas feature alongside artefacts from Danebury hill fort at Andover's Museum of the Iron Age. Together with material from other local sites, the museum tells the story of Hampshire life in the Iron Age and Roman periods. There's also a gift shop and light refreshments.

ODIHAM AND THE BASINGSTOKE CANAL

DISTANCE/TIME	4.5 miles (7.3km) / 2hrs 15mins
ASCENT/GRADIENT	164ft (50m) / ▲
PATHS	Canal towpath, field edge and woodland, 4 stiles
LANDSCAPE	Farmland, parkland, woodland and residential area
SUGGESTED MAP	OS Explorer 144 Basingstoke, Alton & Whitchurch
START/FINISH	Grid reference: SU741510
DOG FRIENDLINESS	May need lifting over some stiles; keep under control in fields
PARKING	Odiham High Street or signed pay-and-display car parks
PUBLIC TOILETS	None on route

Flanked by the expanding towns of Aldershot and Basingstoke, and the M3, Odiham retains an unspoilt, country-town atmosphere and is one of Hampshire's most elegant small towns. Handsome Georgian houses and colour-washed, timber-framed cottages line the wide main street, including The George Hotel (now Bel and the Dragon at The George), first licensed in 1540, and Kingston House, built in the 18th century of local brick in Flemish bond. Some highlights include the 14th-century church, The Bury with its stocks and whipping post, and it's also worth seeing the Tudor vicarage.

Canal link to London

Inextricably linked with the town is the Basingstoke Canal. When it opened in 1794, Odiham Wharf saw shipments of timber, grain, malt, coal and various manufactured goods. This once-popular commercial route, linking London with North Hampshire, climbed through Surrey via 29 locks. The waterway also had 69 bridges, two aqueducts, active wharfs and warehouses and, at 37 miles (59.5km), was the longest canal in southern England.

The coming of the railways led to its gradual decline, although it was used to transport materials for the construction of Aldershot Garrison in the 1850s and for shifting munitions during World War I. During World War II, the canal formed a useful lowland link in a line of defence created between Margate and Bristol. Following a period of restoration, 32 miles (51.5km) of the canal reopened as a leisure amenity in 1991.

Many regard the canal as a linear country park. The clean spring water supply harbours a rich wildlife and forms one of Britain's finest areas for aquatic plants. Surprisingly though, the canal is more famous for bats. The partially collapsed 1,230yd (1,125m) Greywell Tunnel — home to some 12,500 bats of all native species, including Natterer's and Daubenton's bats — is the largest bat roost in Britain. Return to the tunnel entrance at dusk to watch the spectacle of thousands of bats leaving to feed. Set adjacent to the tow path you'll also see the picturesque ruins of King John's Castle, sometimes known as Odiham Castle. Built in 1212, it was used by King John as a resting place between Windsor and Winchester.

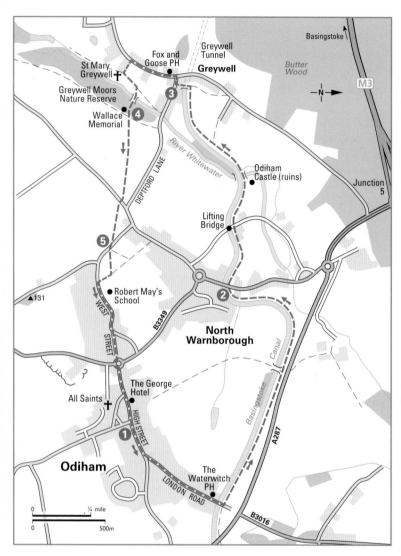

1. Head east along the High Street and take the left fork, London Road, leading to the Basingstoke Canal. Pass The Waterwitch pub and cross the bridge, then drop down left to the towpath. Follow the waterway signed to Odiham Castle/ deer park, parallel with the A287 for just over a mile (1.6km) to North Warnborough.

2. Keep on the towpath, passing under the road bridge and then a lifting bridge, and after 300yds (274m) pass the ruins of Odiham Castle (also known

as King John's Castle) on your right. Pass over the River Whitewater and continue for half a mile (800m) to Greywell Tunnel, famous for its roosting bat population and best visited at dusk, when the bats take to the air. Take the path left over its portal and drop down to the road.

3. Turn right onto Deptford Lane and after a few paces left onto The Street at the junction to pass The Fox and Goose. Walk through the village and turn left through the lychgate to St Mary Greywell church. Walk down the path to the church and turn left through the kissing gate opposite the main door. Walk across the field for 180yds (165m) to a stile; now turn right to a second stile on the edge of the trees and take the bridge to cross over the River Whitewater and enter Greywell Moors Nature Reserve.

4. Go ahead through a kissing gate. Walk through the reserve, passing a memorial to the eminent botanist E C Wallace to another kissing gate. Enter a field and bear slightly left to walk in an easterly direction across the field to the road. Turn left for 50yds (46m), then right with the footpath sign just before a private driveway. After a few paces, turn left through a gap in the hedge, then bear diagonally across a paddock and keep ahead across the next field to leave the field through a gap in the hedge and the road.

5. Cross to the stile opposite and walk across the field, heading to a stile. Join a path beside Robert May's School, turning right to reach West Street. Turn left, passing the school, then, as the road veers left, bear right up West Street to the roundabout. Bear right to the crossing then continue back along Odiham High Street.

Where to eat and drink

Odiham has a good range of pubs and restaurants and a number of tempting cafés. There's also the Fox and Goose pub in Greywell.

What to see

The tow path is a good place for birding. You may see mallards, wagtails, herons, little grebe, summer migrants like spotted flycatchers, willow warblers and swallows and, if you're lucky, the blue flash of a kingfisher. Dragonflies and butterflies abound and you may also spot a pike feeding in the shallows.

While you're there

Stroll around Odiham. Behind All Saints church and near the almshouses built in 1625 is a pest house of about the same date. Constructed to isolate suspected sufferers of the plague until they recovered or died, this fine example is one of only a handful that survive in Hampshire and is open to visitors at weekends. In the churchyard are the graves of several French prisoners. They were held at a camp in an old chalk pit on the Alton road during the Napoleonic War and it is thought they helped build the Basingstoke Canal.

WHITCHURCH AND THE RIVER TEST

DISTANCE/TIME	5.5 miles (8.8km) / 2hrs 45min
ASCENT/GRADIENT	351ft (107m) / ▲
PATHS	Riverside paths, field-edge paths and road
LANDSCAPE	Town streets and farmland
SUGGESTED MAP	OS Explorer 144 Basingstoke, Alton & Whitchurch
START/FINISH	Grid reference: SU463478
DOG FRIENDLINESS	Keep dogs under control at all times
PARKING	Car park at Gill Nethercott Centre, next to Whitchurch Silk Mill on Winchester Street
PUBLIC TOILETS	Bell Street, Whitchurch

Whitchurch was first established as a borough and a market town in the 13th century because of its location at a crossing point on the River Test and a junction of two major routes. This small town was at its most important during the coaching era, when it was the first overnight stop out of London. Industry, in the form of mills, flourished in the town and along the Test, utilising the river to provide power before electricity.

The Silk Mill, which straddles the Test, survives and is a splendid example of industrial architecture. Built in 1815 on the site of previous mills, it was used for hand-weaving wool before switching to silk weaving around 1830. You can visit the Silk Mill before or after your walk but it is not the only mill you will see along the route.

Making money

The iron-free water of the infant River Test is ideal for papermaking, notably for the manufacture of watermarked banknote paper, and several local mills grew up to further this industry. Henri Portal, a Huguenot from France, first established his papermaking business at Bere Mill in 1712. It has been a pictureque spot ever since but, alas, much of this weatherboarded mill was destroyed by fire in early 2018 and is currently undergoing renovation.

Portal moved to his new mill at Laverstoke in 1724, where he started making the watermarked paper for banknotes. The brand name of Portals had, and still has, a monopoly in this specialised type of paper and the original contract with the Bank of England survives to this day. The business remained in Laverstoke until 1950, when it moved to a mill in nearby Overton, which Portals had opened in 1922. The old paper mill now houses another valuable commodity, the Bombay Sapphire Gin Distillery.

Much of the estate village at Laverstoke was built by Portals for its workers. Look out for the unusual row of half-thatched cottages, built in 1939 in an Arts and Crafts style, and the finely built, ochre-coloured Laverstoke House, built in 1796 for Harry Portal.

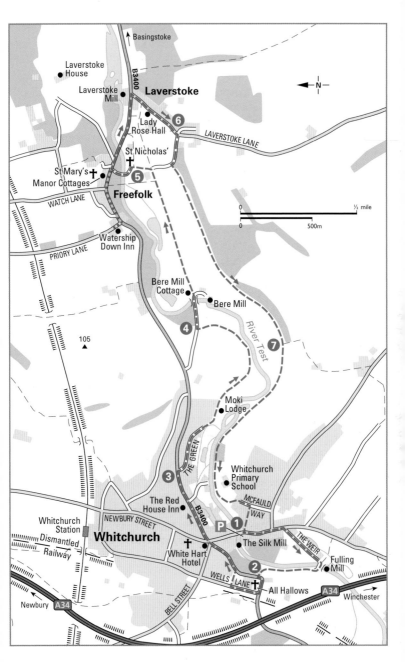

1. Turn right along the Winchester road, then right again at The Weir. Follow the lane past some allotments on the left to one of the many old watermills in this area, Grade II-listed Fulling Mill. Cross the stream and then turn right down the waymarked path to cross the river, and follow the footpath beside the River Test.

2. At the road, bear sharp left up to All Hallows church and turn right onto Wells Lane. Just before the railway bridge, turn right down Fairclose and continue down the footpath. Turn left at the bottom, towards the village centre. At the mini-roundabout, take the road to the right of The White Hart, to 'Overton'.

3. After 0.25 miles (400m), turn right down The Green, the road narrowing to a track by the wooden Moki Lodge. Go through a gate and follow the fenced path along the left-hand edge of water-meadows. Bear left through a hedge and follow the right-hand field edge, which soon swings left beside the River Test. Go through a kissing gate, signed 'Mill Trail', and bear slightly left across a field to another kissing gate and a metalled drive.

4. Turn right, cross the bridge beside Bere Mill Cottage and keep left at a fork of footpaths to a gate. Go through, and up to a kissing gate. Bear slightly right across the field to a kissing gate and pass a bench. Keep ahead along the right-hand field boundary, then head right and continue ahead to a kissing gate. Turn left and follow a gravel track to visit St Nicholas' church.

5. Leave the churchyard and bear right down a road, following it right over the River Test to the B3400. Cross to the pavement opposite and turn left here, opposite Manor Cottages, and continue for 200yds (183m) for the Watership Down Inn; otherwise turn right and cross the river. Turn right, opposite Laverstoke Mill, along Laverstoke Lane and pass Lady Rose Hall.

6. As the road starts to bend, turn right along a track, following blue way-markers (for the Mill Trail). Climb steadily then, as it turns sharp right, bear left alongside a field and follow the field edge left to a gap in the far corner. Pass through a kissing gate into another field, keeping to the left and gradually descend to the gate in the corner, and continue beside the woods to a further gate (ignore the stile to your left).

7. Keep ahead beneath a steep wooded bank on your left. Go through a wooden gate at a break in the trees and then through a kissing gate. Continue along the right-hand edge of two fields, with the river on your right. Keep ahead through woodland and then beside another field. After leaving the field, bear right in a meadow and pass a wooden seat near the back of the school. Bear left on a metalled footpath, pass the school gate and skirt the playing fields. Follow McFauld Way ahead and turn right opposite Alliston Way along a path beside playing fields and down an alleyway. Cross the road at the bottom to return to the car park.

Where to eat and drink

Whitchurch has a good choice of pubs, notably The Red House Inn and the White Hart Hotel. Home-made lunches, tea and coffee are available in the Silk Mill Tearoom (admission charge). The Watership Down Inn at Freefolk offers a full restaurant-style menu.

What to see

All Hallows church in Whitchurch has some interesting memorials, particularly a fine brass of Richard Brooke and family (1603).

EXPLORING
HAREWOOD FOREST

DISTANCE/TIME	7.9 miles (12.7km) / 3hrs 30min
ASCENT/GRADIENT	525ft (160m) / ▲ ▲
PATHS	Field, woodland paths and tracks, 3 stiles
LANDSCAPE	Water-meadow, rolling farmland and thick woodland
SUGGESTED MAP	OS Explorer 131 Romsey, Andover & Test Valley
START/FINISH	Grid reference: SU426439
DOG FRIENDLINESS	Can run free through Harewood Forest
PARKING	Car park at St Nicholas church or by village hall
PUBLIC TOILETS	None on route

Hidden away in the heart of Harewood Forest, at an eerie place called Deadman's Plack, is a solitary pink granite cross. Despite standing over 70ft (21m) tall, it's shrouded by trees and can be difficult to find. The reasons for its construction will send shivers down your spine.

Colonel Iremonger, owner of Wherwell Priory, erected the monument in 1825 to commemorate the spot where Edgar, grandson of Alfred the Great and King of England, is supposed to have murdered his friend Athelwold in AD 963. The events leading to this bloody deed make a classic tale of love, jealousy and hate. Eager to marry again following the death of his first wife, Edgar sent one of his trusted courtiers, Earl Athelwold, to visit Elfrida, daughter of Ordgar, Earl of Devon, to see if the reports of her beauty were true. But Althelwold fell in love with her and, before wooing and marrying her, sent back a message that she was ugly and would be unsuitable as a queen. Edgar soon found out he had been deceived and Elfrida, having realised that she had lost her chance at becoming queen, turned her charms towards Edgar. The king too was smitten and fell in love. He could not forgive Athelwold and it is said that Edgar and Elfrida plotted together to murder him. Edgar invited the earl on a hunting trip in Harewood Forest and at Deadman's Plack stabbed him to death. He promptly married Elfrida and they had a son, Ethelred. Following the King's death in AD 975, his son Edward from his first marriage succeeded him to the throne. Jealous of her stepson and anxious for her own son Ethelred to be king, Elfrida stabbed Edward to death at Corfe Castle in AD 978. However, stricken with remorse, she founded a nunnery on the banks of the River Test at Wherwell, 3 miles (4.8km) south of Deadman's Plack. Haunted by her own conscience she lived a life of penitence until her death in 1002.

Leaving the Deadman's Plack copse behind you, the walk soon merges with the Test Way. This well waymarked trail leads you back into the Test Valley and Longparish. Stretching for 3 miles (4.8km) along the River Test, the village was originally known as Middleton before its name was superseded by its nickname 'Longparish'.

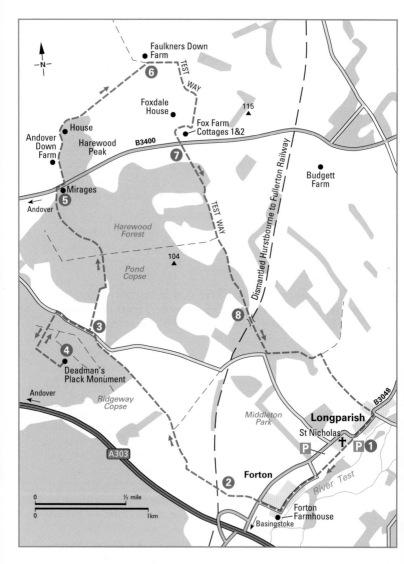

1. Walk through the churchyard, exit via the gate opposite the main door and turn right to follow the Test Way (TW) across the water-meadow. Go through two gates and bear left along the lane into the village of Forton. Go round the sharp right-hand bend by a barn at Forton Farmhouse to a T-junction. Pass through the gate opposite to a path running diagonally across the field, then bear right along a rough track.

2. Cross the course of the old Hurstbourne-to-Fullerton branch line, then keep ahead beside a low hedge on your right. Go through a gap in the top corner of the field, then bear right at a marker post, still following the hedge on your right. Continue into the next field and follow the waymarked path to the left of a small wood, ignoring the main track forking to the right. Shortly, cross a

track to follow the path along the left-hand edge of a large field at the base of a shallow valley. On reaching the field corner, keep ahead through trees to a lane and left turn.

3. To visit Deadman's Plack follow the lane for 500yds (457m). Turn left over a stile and cross the meadow into woods. Keep ahead over a concrete track, then drop gently to another concrete track and turn left along the signed 'Permissive footpath to the monument'. After 110yds (100m) turn left to reach the monument hidden in the trees.

4. Retrace your steps back to just before Point 3. Turn left, then cross the stile in the hedge on the left and follow a path between fields and then alongside woodland. Bear left by a marker post to join the main track through Harewood Forest. Keep ahead at a crossing of paths by a large conifer tree and eventually join a gravel drive to the B3400.

5. Turn right, then almost immediately left up the drive to Andover Down Farm. Keep to the right of the farm and a small industrial site. Bear off the drive, left at gates to a house and follow the track right. Head downhill towards Faulkners Down Farm.

6. At the farm, bear right along its drive, in front of the house. Proceed downhill, turning right off the road at the 'Private Road, No Thoroughfare' sign on to the TW, a track between fields. Go through a gap in the hedge (TW), and then follow the left-hand field-edge to a gap near cottages. Bear left on the drive to the B3400.

7. Cross the road and go through the gap in the hedge opposite to follow the grassy track (TW) beside rolling arable land. Gently climb, then descend, to join a stony track, coming from the right, beneath the beech canopy. Shortly, bear left (TW) along a track to a metalled track.

8. Bear left along the track, cross over the old railway on a bridge and then continue onto a metalled driveway. Keep left at a fork and continue ahead when the metalled surface becomes a gravel track. Follow this left and out of the woods to shortly reach a junction of tracks. Turn right (TW) to Longparish. At the village lane, turn right, back to the church or village hall.

Where to eat and drink

There is nowhere to eat on the walk but The Cricketers Inn, about half a mile (800m) further up the B3048 from the church car park, has a good menu, with roasts or barbecues on Sundays.

What to see

You will cross the former track of the Hurstbourne-to-Fullerton branch railway. Built in 1885, it connected with the London-to-Salisbury line and was a favourite with Queen Victoria, who asked to take the line whenever she travelled to Southampton, en route to Osborne House. Passenger trains ceased running in 1931, although freight trains used the line until 1956, including those that carried ammunition during World War II to Harewood Forest where it was stored.

ADVENTURES IN THE CANDOVERS

DISTANCE/TIME	2.4 miles (3.8km) / 1hr
ASCENT/GRADIENT	151ft (46m) / ▲
PATHS	Mostly firm tree-shaded tracks, with initial roadside section (no pavement)
LANDSCAPE	Gently undulating arable farmland
SUGGESTED MAP	OS Explorer OL32 Winchester, New Alresford & East Meon
START/FINISH	Grid reference: SU578393
DOG FRIENDLINESS	Keep on lead (shooting country)
PARKING	Roadside lay-by on B3046, centre of Brown Candover
PUBLIC TOILETS	None on route

Walking up beside the cricket field towards the trim and neatly kept church of St Peter and its impressive row of yew trees, the words 'media frenzy' and 'Brown Candover' seem unlikely bedfellows. And yet, in 1928, correspondents from titles as diverse as *The Times* and the *Children's Newspaper* converged on the Candover Valley. Television was still in the future but Brown Candover was featured on the radio and in local papers from as far away as Yorkshire and Chiswick.

Old William's tale

The seeds of this story were sown in the 19th century, when the parish of Brown Candover had been merged with neighbouring Chilton Candover. The little church at Chilton Candover was declared redundant and was pulled down in 1876 — and over the years, the old churchyard became overgrown and neglected. When the rector, Reverend Gough, decided to tidy it up, he struck up a conversation with 80-year-old William Spiers who had lived in the village all his life. Old William told the rector that he remembered kicking skulls around in 'a great old place' underneath the churchyard when he was a boy.

In the best traditions of Victorian amateur archaeology, Reverend Gough called in his son and the two men started to dig. The press was quick to catch on. Was it an underground church? A Roman temple? Everyone seemed to have different ideas, though the structure was eventually identified as a Norman crypt with a barrel-vaulted nave and lancet windows. Inside the crypt was the 14th-century tomb of John of Candover.

A Victorian replacement

The little building is on private land but you'll see its successor easily enough on this walk. Largely financed by the wealthy Baring banking family who lived at nearby Northington Grange, St Peter's church was built in 1844. It was designed by T H Wyatt, who later worked on new assize courts in Winchester and went on to become President of the Royal Institute of British Architects.

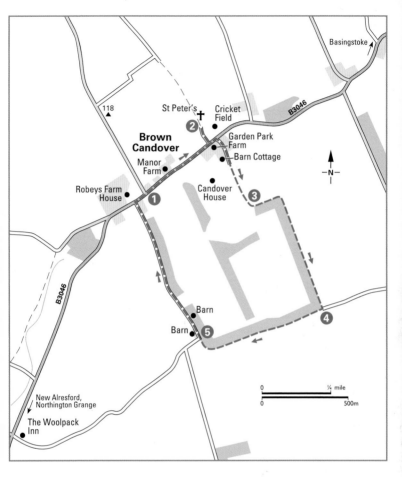

1. Turn right out of the layby and walk northeast along the B3046, leaving the Woodmancott turning behind you. Follow the flint wall of Manor Farm on the left, then pass the gates of Candover House on the right. Turn left onto the Wayfarer's Walk opposite Garden Park Farm and walk up the side of the cricket field to visit the church.

2. Return to the road and turn left and then right onto the restricted byway. Pass Barn Cottage and its large black barn and continue along the firm track, with glimpses of the impressive 18th-century Candover House through the hedge on your right.

3. Turn left at the top corner of the field, keeping the line of trees on your right, then follow the track as it swings to the right and continue up the gentle slope, ignoring the gap in the hedge to the left, to a T-junction.

4. Turn right onto the waymarked off-road cycle trail that runs along the Ox Drove. The track follows a large field on the left, before bending sharply right to reach a junction by some large modern barns and a metalled road going to the left.

5. Keep ahead past the barns onto a surfaced farm lane and continue down the hill to the B3046, with the handsome frontage of Robeys Farm House ahead. Turn right at the bottom to complete the short distance back to your car.

Where to eat and drink

Local produce features strongly at the stylish Woolpack Inn in Totford, just down the road towards Alresford. Children are welcome and there's a pleasant garden with a children's play area for warmer days. Palmers Dorset ales and Marstons support the blackboard and dining room menus, which include bar snacks, pub classics and à la carte options, as well as traditional roasts on Sundays.

What to see

Mounted on the west wall of St Peter's church, just inside the main door, you'll find a monumental brass dating back to the reign of Henry VIII. The brass, which came from the old church and was placed here in 1889, is unusual because the two figures are standing arm in arm.

While you're there

Visit Northington Grange for an idea of the family that built St Peter's church. The building that you'll see was converted from an earlier house with the addition of classical Greek facades shortly before the Baring family bought it in 1817. Alexander Baring was created Lord Ashburton in 1835 and the family continued to adapt the house throughout the 19th century. The house was sold before World War II and suffered years of neglect after its last owner died in 1964. The present guardian of the building, English Heritage, has made many improvements since taking over the property in 1975 and today the building hosts an annual opera festival.

A LOOP AROUND ALICE HOLT FOREST

DISTANCE/TIME	2.5 miles (4km) / 1 hour 15 min
ASCENT/GRADIENT	197ft (60m) / ▲ ▲
PATHS	Well-marked tracks and woodland paths, muddy in places, several flights of steps
LANDSCAPE	Undulating mixed woodland
SUGGESTED MAP	AA Walker's Map 23 Guildford, Farnham & The Downs
START/FINISH	Grid reference: SU811415
DOG FRIENDLINESS	Popular for dogs
PARKING	ANPR (pay on exit) car park
PUBLIC TOILETS	In the visitor centre

There's been a forest at Alice Holt since about 5000 BC. Iron Age people were using the local clay, water and fuel to make pottery here in the 1st century BC and those potteries expanded into a major industry in the years following the Roman invasion.

Many of the trees had already been felled to fuel the pottery kilns by the time the Romans left, early in the 5th century. The Saxons continued the felling, this time to create fields for their crops, but by the Middle Ages Alice Holt had become a royal hunting forest governed by a strict legal code. In later centuries more timber was extracted for construction and shipbuilding, so that by 1655 Charles II ordered the woods to be replanted. The forest's heartbeat is measured in decades and the trees grew quietly for more than 100 years until the Napoleonic Wars once again created a demand for shipbuilding timber.

Replanting a forest

The modern history of Alice Holt really began after the Enclosure Act of 1812, when 1,600 acres (648ha) were enclosed and once again replanted with oak. By the time those trees came to maturity Britain was in the thick of World War I and the coal mines and trenches were swallowing up vast quantities of timber for pit props and revetments. Timber was a scarce commodity in post-war Britain and the government set up the Forestry Commission to help boost the supply of home-grown timber.

The new agency took over responsibility for Alice Holt in 1924 and set about planting quick-growing conifers to meet the demand. Following World War II, the Forestry Commission began developing a research station around Alice Holt Lodge to the west of the A325 and additional laboratories were built in the late 1970s. Today, the Commission's scientists are working on topical issues like environmental change, as well as exploring potential sources of biomass energy.

But, as you'll see from the picnic areas and play structures along this route, recreation facilities have also become a key part of the forest.

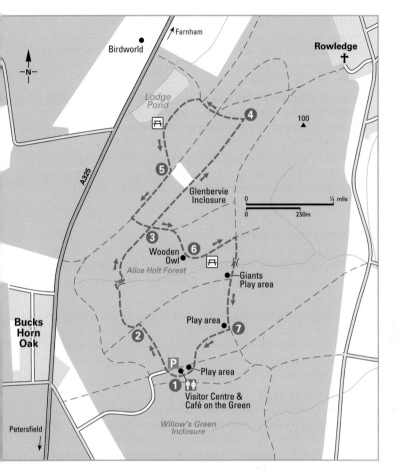

1. Walk through the car park from the visitor centre and turn left at the purple waymarker post (Lodge Pond Trail – LPT) opposite the large central fingerpost and signboard. Keep ahead past the turning on your left and descend to a forest track.

2. Turn left along LPT for 45yds (41m), then turn right down the steps, cross a brook and climb the steps on the other side. Follow the winding trail past a bench seat and down the steps to cross a stream. Bear left beyond the steps on the other side, climbing steadily on the undulating route before the path levels out to a crossways by a bench.

3. Keep ahead (purple arrow), pass a seat and then a clearing on the left and keep ahead. Climb steadily to a purple waymarker post (LPT) indicating a narrow woodland path off to your left.

4. Turn left here, and left at the T-junction (on LPT). Continue to a five-way junction by a bench and keep ahead across the broad forest track, waymarked towards Lodge Pond. Keep ahead at the next junction and turn left to walk parallel with the edge of the pond. Bear left past picnic tables, then turn right through a small parking area to a T-junction at the top of the clearing.

5. Turn right (on LPT) onto the forest track and continue for 500yds (457m) to a waymarked junction. Turn left, following the purple arrow, and keep ahead at the crossways that you passed earlier (Point 3), then take the right-hand turning (following the purple arrow) onto a path that leads down to a large wooden owl play structure.

6. Turn left at the wooden owl, now following the yellow arrow (Habitat Trail) and pass the picnic table and another play structure, then turn right at the crossways (yellow arrow). Cross a stream, pass the Giants Play Area, and keep left (purple arrow), then climb almost to the crest of the hill.

7. Turn right (purple arrow), pass another play area, bear left and across a track, then turn right past more play equipment to reach the forest centre. Turn right past the Café on the Green and walk back to the car park.

Where to eat and drink

The Café on the Green is right next to the car park and opens daily for drinks, ice creams and hot and cold food to eat in or take away. Expect sandwiches, paninis, all-day breakfast, soup and jacket potatoes.

What to see

The woodlands at Alice Holt are managed for their wildlife. You might see birds like the lesser-spotted woodpecker, nightjar or willow tit, as well as the purple emperor butterfly, which is the emblem of Alice Holt Forest. Perhaps more obviously, large mammals including muntjac and roe deer live in the woods.

While you're there

Just up the road towards Farnham is Birdworld, an extensive family attraction with exotic birds and animals, a farm and an aquarium. There are keeper-led bird shows, and feeding times to admire the penguins are a top attraction. There is also a Go Ape aerial adventure playground at Alice Holt.

JANE AUSTEN'S CHAWTON

DISTANCE/TIME	5.8 miles (9.4km) / 2hrs 45min
ASCENT/GRADIENT	226ft (69m) / ▲
PATHS	Field paths, old railway track, some road walking, 14 stiles
LANDSCAPE	Gently rolling farmland interspersed with woodland
SUGGESTED MAP	OS Explorer OL33 Haslemere & Petersfield
START/FINISH	Grid reference: SU708375
DOG FRIENDLINESS	Keep dogs under control at all times
PARKING	Free village car park opposite Jane Austen's House Museum
PUBLIC TOILETS	None; walkers may use toilets at Jane Austen's House Museum

Devoted followers of Jane Austen know and revere the village of Chawton, a quiet backwater off the A31 south of Alton, for it was here that she spent the last eight years of her life and where she wrote her major works. Since the dramatisation of her novels, interest in her personal life has increased and the village and her home have become internationally famous.

Jane Austen's house

Jane Austen was born in Steventon, near Basingstoke, and spent the first 25 years of her life there before the family moved to Bath in 1801. Following spells in Clifton and Southampton, she moved to Chawton Cottage with her mother and sister Cassandra in July 1809. Her house, now called Jane Austen's House Museum, belonged to her brother Edward, who had inherited the estate of Chawton from his uncle Thomas Knight, whose family had purchased the manor in 1578. It was Edward who renovated the building, adding three further bedrooms so that his mother and sisters could live in comfort and entertain friends. Jane wrote about the cottage to her brother Francis Austen in 1809:

'Our Chawton House, how much we find/Already in it to our mind:/And convinced, that when complete/It will all other houses beat/That ever have been made or mended/With rooms concise and rooms distended.'

It was at Chawton Cottage that she spent her most active writing phase. At a small table in the living room she began to revise her earlier manuscript novels – *Sense and Sensibility*, *Pride and Prejudice* and *Northanger Abbey* – and then wrote her great novels *Mansfield Park*, *Emma* and *Persuasion*. Jane became ill in 1816 and moved to Winchester to seek medical advice. She died in 1817 aged 41 and is buried in Winchester Cathedral.

You can visit the charming red-brick house which has been beautifully restored to look as it would have done in the 1800s. It is more than a museum, it succeeds in capturing the atmosphere of her modest lifestyle through collections of family mementoes and documentary material which give a real insight into her life and writings. View the drawing room, the parlour where she wrote her novels, and the bedrooms, then browse in the bookshop and enjoy a picnic in the flower-filled garden.

Tea at Farringdon

The walk explores some of the peaceful open countryside through which Jane Austen would have strolled. The furthest point on the walk is Upper Farringdon. She often visited the village to see Harriet Benn, whose father was the vicar of All Saints Church. 'Harriet Benn,' she wrote, 'sleeps at the Great House (Chawton House) to-night and spends to-morrow with us; and the plan is that we should all walk with her to drink tea at Faringdon'.

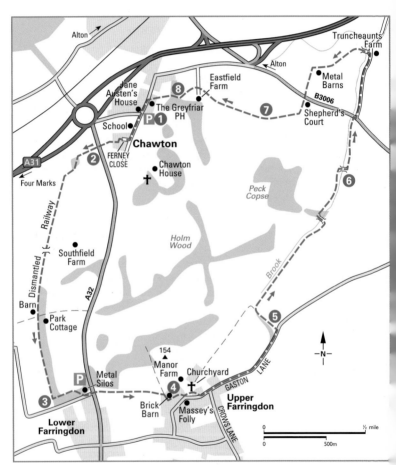

1. Turn left out of the car park, opposite Jane Austen's House Museum, and walk along a dead-end lane. Pass the school and turn right into Ferney Close. Keep to the left and bear left along a path beside Ferney Bungalow on St Swithuns Way to a gate. Go through the gate and continue along the enclosed path to a stile, then descend steps and cross (with care) the A32.

2. Climb steps, directly opposite, go through a metal kissing gate and walk along the left-hand field edge, leading to a stile on your left. Go through a copse, following the path right, then left, between fields. Keep straight ahead along a former railway track, go under a brick-arch bridge, and continue for 650yds (594m) beyond the barn near Park Cottage.

3. Just before a second arch, bear left off the old railway line and follow the field edge until it heads right into the trees and then left on a metalled drive-way. Cross the A32 again and join a track leading to Manor Farm. At a crossing of tracks, just before a barn with solar panels on its roof, turn right alongside a children's play area. Take the narrow path left at the bottom of the play area to reach a track.

4. Turn right to the lane in Upper Farringdon, opposite Massey's Folly. Turn left into the churchyard and leave by the main gate, turning left along the lane. Keep ahead along Church Road and then Gaston Lane for half a mile (800m) to a signposted track on your left.

5. Turn left, then soon take the grassy track right, just before the track bends left. Climb the stile ahead into open pasture, following the brook on your left, under the power lines, to a second stile; after 170yds (155m) cross the bridge over the brook on your left. Keep going, with the brook to your right, to a stile at the end of the field.

6. Turn right to cross the brook, and follow it left to the road, crossing a stile to reach the B3006. Turn right, then cross the road to join a tarmac track and follow it to Truncheaunts Farm. Cross the stile, on the left at the fingerpost, opposite the drive up to the farmhouse, and then cross the footbridge, and follow the right-hand field edge, between two fences. Bear left past the metal barn and follow the track towards the B3006. Bear right through a gap, cross the drive and a stile. Go through the gap to the road, opposite Shepherd's Court. Cross over, and through a gate, walk down a concrete track, and turn right through a gate at the end. Follow the right-hand field edge to a gate.

7. Bear right across the field to reach two stiles set in the hedge and bear slightly left across three more fields and stiles towards Eastfield Farm. Cross the drive and pass through a kissing gate, walking through a field to reach a gate beside woodland.

8. Follow the path straight down through the copse to a metal kissing gate. Bear slightly left across a field to a further stile. Continue ahead to a metal kissing gate in the wall and take the narrow footpath back to the main village street. Turn left to the car park.

Where to eat and drink

Opposite Jane Austen's House Museum you'll find Cassandra's Cup, renowned for home-baked cakes, cream teas and hot savoury snacks at lunchtime (seasonal opening). A few doors down is The Greyfriar pub (open all day), with its sheltered garden, offering traditional meals and daily specials.

What to see

You can't really miss Massey's Folly, an enormous red-brick building, in Upper Farringdon. Designed and built over a period of 30 years by Thomas Massey, who served as rector in the village for 62 years, it is probably the strangest building in Hampshire. With 17 bedrooms and two towers, its purpose is unknown, but since 1925 has been used as a school and village hall. In 2015 it was sold to be developed into housing. The eccentric Massey is buried just outside the church porch.

While you're there

Explore the Elizabethan mansion of Chawton House, with its fine collection of literary works by early women writers in the Library. Edward Austen, Jane Austen's brother, was adopted into the Knight family, who owned it, at the age of 16. He later managed the estate, and this connection enabled him to let a house in the village to his mother and sisters, Jane and Cassandra. Visits to library and house are by guided tour on selected weekdays, but you can also ramble in the beautifully restored gardens.

SELBORNE — IN GILBERT WHITE'S FOOTSTEPS

DISTANCE/TIME	3.7 miles (5.9km) / 2hrs
ASCENT/GRADIENT	719ft (219m) / ▲ ▲
PATHS	Woodland, field paths, stretch of road, 7 stiles
LANDSCAPE	Lofty beech hangers, lush rolling pasture and woodland
SUGGESTED MAP	OS Explorer OL33 Haslemere & Petersfield
START/FINISH	Grid reference: SU742334
DOG FRIENDLINESS	Dogs should be kept under control at all times
PARKING	Free National Trust car park behind The Selborne Arms
PUBLIC TOILETS	At car park in Selborne

Selborne, and its beautiful surrounding countryside, were made famous over two centuries ago by the writings and reputation of the clergyman and pioneer naturalist Gilbert White who published *The Natural History and Antiquities of Selborne* in 1789. Based on 40 years of observation and meticulous recording of the flora and fauna around the village, it is one of the few books on natural history to gain the rank of an English classic. White poetically describes his day-to-day experiences of nature in the Hampshire countryside through a series of letters to his friends Thomas Pennant and Daines Barrington.

Local boy
Born in the village in 1720, White was the grandson of the vicar of Selborne, and, having been ordained after attending Oxford, he returned to live in the village to serve as a curate at neighbouring parishes and at Selborne in 1751. From the age of ten until his death in 1793 he lived at The Wakes, a large rambling house that overlooks the village green (the Plestor) and church.

Although the village has changed, White would find the surrounding landscape that he knew and loved so well largely unspoilt and now preserved by the National Trust. This walk literally follows in White's footsteps, exploring the lofty, beech-clad hills or 'hangers' that rise steeply behind his home, and the lush 'lythes' or meadows beyond St Mary's church, both beautiful areas through which he would stroll and passionately observe and note the wildlife around him. The walk comprises two loops around the village, so if you are short of time (or energy) you can enjoy the classic climb on to Selborne Common and still have time to visit Gilbert White's home, now a museum.

Up the Zig-Zag path
The walk begins with a long ascent to the top of Selborne Hill and Common, made easier by the work of Gilbert White and his brother John in 1753, when they constructed the Zig-Zag path up the steep scarp face. White described the Common as 'a vast hill of chalk, rising three hundred feet above the village; and is divided into a sheep down, the high wood, and a long hanging wood

called The Hanger'. You are rewarded with peace and tranquillity when you reach White's Wishing Stone, and magnificent views over the village.

The main route threads through the glorious beech hangers to White's favourite viewpoint. Back in the village, locate White's grave in the churchyard and visit St Mary's church. Here you will find White's fine memorial window depicting St Francis of Assisi preaching to 82 birds, which are mentioned in his book. The second loop heads east through the Oakhanger Valley, following the Hangers Way to Priory Farm, the site of Selborne Priory.

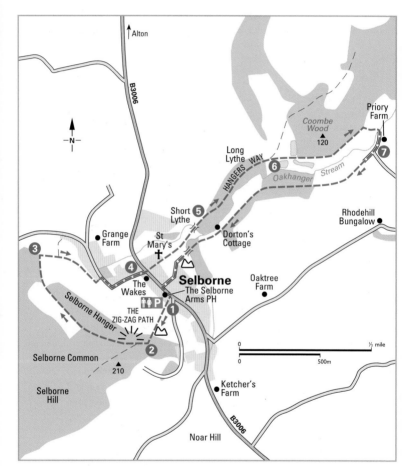

1. Take the arrowed footpath, signed 'Zig Zag Selborne Common', by the car park entrance, and gently ascend to a gate at the base of Selborne Common. Bear left to follow the impressive Zig-Zag path uphill, pausing at regular intervals to admire the unfolding view across the village. At a T-junction near a metal bench turn left to continue upward on the steps.

2. At the top, take the stepped path right and, in a few paces, keep right at a fork to follow the lower path through the beech hangers. Shortly after, look for a metal bench by a path ascending from the right, and savour the splendid

view of the church and The Wakes through the gap in the trees. Continue along the main path, descending to a junction of paths, by a National Trust sign.

3. Turn right along a track, then, where this curves left, bear off right across a stile into pasture. Keep to the left-hand edge, cross three more stiles and follow the enclosed path to a lane. Turn right and follow it back into the village.

4. Cross the B3006 up a gravel driveway and through the right-hand gate into the churchyard. Follow the defined path, marked as Hangers Way, to a footbridge over the Oakhanger Stream.

5. Keep to the Hangers Way through a gate and along the edge of meadowland to a pair of kissing gates, then enter the Long Lythe and pass below a stretch of woodland to a kissing gate and fork of paths, which is within 22yds (20m) of entering the meadow.

6. Fork right leaving the Hangers Way and passing between ponds. Eventually pass alongside a fence to a stile on the edge of Coombe Wood. Turn left over a stile and then over a plank bridge. Follow the path inside the wood to another stile, then bear left along the field edge to a metal kissing gate and turn right along a bridleway towards Priory Farm. Go through the gate, into the farmyard, and keep to the right through another gate and onto a metalled drive.

7. In a few paces, where the drive curves left, bear right along the waymarked track. Go through a metal gate and follow the grassy track along the left-hand side of the field edge, eventually reaching a gate and woodland. Follow the track (which can be muddy) through beech woodland. Leave the wood, passing a house called Dorton's Cottage, and climb the lane steeply back to Selborne, turning left for the car park.

Where to eat and drink

Delicious light lunches, cakes and afternoon teas can be enjoyed in the civilised Tea Parlour at The Wakes, Gilbert White's house. Alternatively, try the pub, The Selborne Arms, which has a family room, for home-cooked bar food. There is also the Selborne Tea Room.

What to see

Note the trunk of a great yew tree in the churchyard which is estimated to be 1,400 years old. By the time it blew down in 1990 its girth measured 26ft (8m) and was taller than the church. Opposite The Wakes is the old butchers' shop. It was obscured by four lime trees, planted by Gilbert White in 1756, to hide 'the blood and filth' from view as he worked in his parlour, and now only the stumps of two remain. Look for the splendid Victorian iron drinking fountain at the south end of the village. It is in the form of a fierce lion's head flanked by windmills.

While you're there

Visit Gilbert White's house. Learn more about the famous naturalist and visit exhibitions commemorating the naturalist and explorer Francis Oates, who journeyed to South America and South Africa, and Captain Lawrence Oates, who accompanied Scott on his ill-fated expedition to the South Pole in 1911.

BRAMSHOTT, GRAYSHOTT AND LUDSHOTT

DISTANCE/TIME	3.9 miles (6.3km) / 1hr 45min
ASCENT/GRADIENT	502ft (153m) / ▲
PATHS	Woodland paths and heathland tracks, 3 stiles
LANDSCAPE	Wooded valley with lakes. Lofty, heather-covered common with far-reaching view
SUGGESTED MAP	AA Walker's Map 23 Guildford, Farnham & The Downs
START/FINISH	Grid reference: SU855336
DOG FRIENDLINESS	Vast expanse of heathland where dogs can run free
PARKING	Unsurfaced car park on edge of Bramshott Common
PUBLIC TOILETS	None on route

Much of the landscape on either side of the busy A3 is a mini wilderness of bracken and heather-covered commons and deep wooded valleys etched by tiny streams. Surprisingly, this unspoilt area was once the heart of a thriving iron industry, with streams like the Wey and Downwater being dammed to provide power for the great hammers in the 17th-century ironworks. Timber for the furnaces and iron ore were locally plentiful.

The chain of dams and the wooded ponds at Waggoner's Wells were created in 1615 by Henry Hooke, lord of the manor of Bramshott, to supply his iron foundry. Now a beauty spot owned by the National Trust, the three beautiful lakes, surrounded by beech woods and home to a wealth of wildlife, are a delight, especially in the autumn when the colours are magnificent.

Writers and poets

Like the poet Tennyson and the writer Flora Thompson, who loved to stroll beside the pools, you will be immediately charmed by this secluded haven. Tennyson, who rented Grayshott Farm (now Grayshott Hall) in 1867, wrote his famous short ode 'Flower in the Crannied Wall' after pulling a flower from one of the crevices at the wishing well you will pass in the valley bottom.

Flora Thompson lived in both Liphook and Grayshott during her 30 years in Hampshire between 1897 and 1927. She often walked to Waggoner's Wells and Bramshott, returning to Grayshott via Ludshott Common. On these long, inspirational country rambles she would observe and assiduously make notes on the wildlife she encountered. Her detailed nature notes reflecting the changing year appeared in her book *The Peverel Papers*. She also describes her life in the area and many of its inhabitants with great affection in the collection of essays called *Heatherley*,

Thompson 'did not often linger by the lakes' on her Sunday walks, but 'climbed at once by a little sandy track to the heath beyond'. Today, on a summer Sunday, the wooded vale attracts the crowds so, if you are seeking

relative solitude, stride up to the open heath and the deciduous
of Ludshott Common. Here, the sandy paths criss-cross purple h
yellow gorse, and the far-reaching wooded views make the stren
worth the effort. Thompson would certainly have seen stoncha
redpolls and nightingales while walking here, and they still nest on the
margins of the heath.

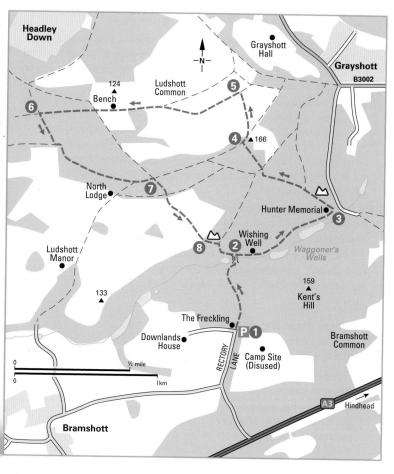

1. From the car park, take the defined path beyond the low barrier and gradually descend. At the bottom, take the main bridleway that directs you left along
a sunken track. (Ignore this if it's wet and muddy and instead climb the drier
path ahead beneath the beech trees.) Follow this track as it bends to the right
then, where the tracks cross, turn left and head down to reach the stream and
a footbridge.

2. Cross the bridge and turn right along the footpath parallel with the stream.
Pass the wishing well and a house and keep to the path, bearing right just
beyond the house, through the valley bottom to the left of three large ponds,
eventually reaching a lane by a ford.

A few steps before the lane, take a sharp left on a bridleway marked Horses', to pass the Hunter memorial stone and then steeply ascend through mixed woodland. As it levels out, cross a path, then a track and soon merge with a wider track. Continue ahead until reaching a gravel cross tracks, and ahead again across a similar track.

4. On meeting the next track, at a T-junction, turn right, emerging from the trees and onto the common at a five-way junction of tracks. Take the second-left track skirting around a clump of gorse and birch trees.

5. Turn left and follow this open heathland trail, edged by bracken and gorse, and eventually merge with a wider sandy trail. Keep left and then, on reaching a bench and junction of ways on the fringe of the common, proceed straight on through the conifer plantation.

6. At a crossing of paths by a line of electricity poles, turn left following the line of the wires. The path bears left and downhill to a cross tracks. Continue ahead on a narrower track through the wood, to emerge beneath the power lines again. Turn left beside some electricity poles and keep ahead for a quarter of a mile (400m), ignoring a bridleway going right, towards North Lodge. Keep ahead with the electricity poles then, after 100yds (91m), turn right at a cross-ways and fingerpost.

7. Turn right and keep straight on at the next crossing of routes, following the footpath alongside a garden to a stile on the woodland edge. Keep ahead between wire fences to a stile on the edge of the wood.

8. Steeply descend into woodland to reach a stile. At the track beyond, turn right downhill to the river and footbridge encountered on the outward route. Retrace your steps back to the car park.

Where to eat and drink

There are no refreshments available on the route but it makes for an ideal morning, afternoon or summer's evening walk, so why not enjoy a picnic beside one of the three delightful ponds at Waggoner's Wells?

What to see

Look out for the memorial stone dedicated to Sir Robert Hunter, a founder of the National Trust who lived in Haslemere. He initiated the local purchase of Hindhead Common before transferring it to the Trust. Walk across Ludshott Common in summer and you may see the dark purplish-brown plumage and the cocked tail of the rare Dartford warbler, and butterflies like the silver-studded blue, grayling and the green hairstreak.

While you're there

Explore Bramshott Common. Grass-covered concrete is all that remains of the huge army camp that stood on either side of the A3 during both World Wars. Bramshott Camp or Mudsplosh Camp and Tin Town, a collection of ramshackle huts and shops built of corrugated iron, housed Canadian soldiers and occupied much of the land here. Visit St Mary's churchyard in Bramshott, which has a special burial ground containing the graves of 350 Canadian soldiers who died during a flu epidemic in 1917.

AROUND THE ALRESFORDS — A WATERCRESS WALK

DISTANCE/TIME	9.4 miles (15.1km) / 3hrs 30min
ASCENT/GRADIENT	833ft (254m) / ▲ ▲
PATHS	Riverside paths, tracks, field, woodland paths and roads
LANDSCAPE	River valley and undulating farmland dotted with woodland
SUGGESTED MAP	OS Explorer OL32 Winchester, New Alresford & East Meon
START/FINISH	Grid reference: SU588325
DOG FRIENDLINESS	Keep dogs under control
PARKING	Pay-and-display car park off Station Road, New Alresford
PUBLIC TOILETS	Station Road, New Alresford

New Alresford (pronounced Allsford) is not very new at all. In fact, this delightful place, one of Hampshire's most picturesque small towns, was 'new' in 1200, when Godfrey de Lucy, Bishop of Winchester, wanted to expand the original Alresford — Old Alresford. He dammed the River Arle, creating a 200-acre (81ha) pond, and built a causeway (the Great Weir) to link Old Alresford with his new community. His 'New Market', as it was first called, thrived to become a prosperous wool town, with a market being held in Broad Street. Most of the medieval timber-framed houses were destroyed by two devastating fires during the 17th century, one in 1644 when the Royalists set the town alight following the Battle of Cheriton. As a result, much of the architecture is Georgian, notably along sumptuous Broad Street, which is lined with lime trees and elegant colour-washed houses. Mary Russell Mitford, the authoress of Our Village which sketches her country life, was born in Broad Street in 1787.

Close to both Old and New Alresford you will find an intricate network of crystal-clear chalk streams, rivulets and channels that form the rivers Arle and Itchen and the Candover Stream. These provide perfect conditions for one of Alresford's major industries, the production of watercress. The watercress beds continue to thrive in this health-conscious age.

The Grange is an important house architecturally, being designed in 1804 by William Wilkins, architect of the National Gallery, in the Greek Revivalist style. The majestic building looks more like a Greek temple, with a Parthenon-like portico supported by two rows of giant Doric columns. It commands a superb position overlooking a lake and rolling parkland. Old Alresford is tiny, with an interesting 18th-century church and two substantial Georgian houses. Make time to visit the church to see the striking monument to Jane Rodney. Admiral Lord Rodney, who is buried in the family vault, built Old Alresford House and is famous for spectacularly defeating the Spanish fleet off Cape St Vincent in 1780.

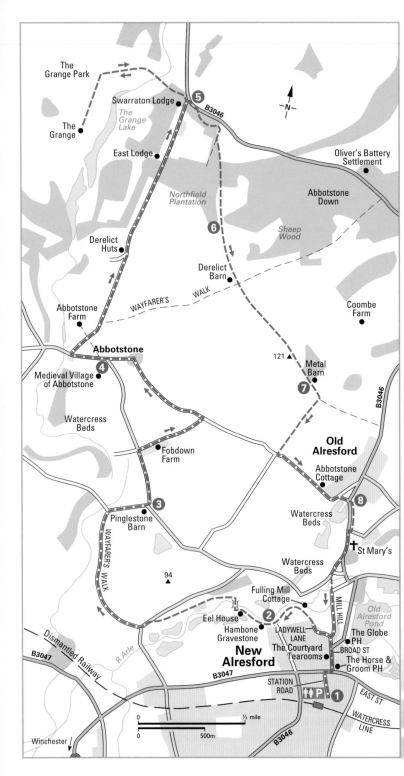

The Grange Park

The Grange

Swarraton Lodge

The Grange Lake

B3046

5

East Lodge

Oliver's Battery Settlement

N

Northfield Plantation

Abbotstone Down

6

Sheep Wood

Derelict Huts

Derelict Barn

Coombe Farm

WAYFARER'S WALK

Abbotstone Farm

Abbotstone

4

Medieval Village of Abbotstone

121 ▲

Metal Barn

7

Watercress Beds

B3046

Old Alresford

Fobdown Farm

Abbotstone Cottage

3

Pinglestone Barn

Watercress Beds

8

WAYFARER'S WALK

St Mary's ✝

94 ▲

Watercress Beds

Fulling Mill Cottage

Old Alresford Pond

MILL HILL

Dismantled Railway

R Arle

Eel House

Hambone Gravestone

2

LADYWELL LANE

New Alresford

The Courtyard Tearooms

The Globe PH

BROAD ST

The Horse & Groom PH

B3047

STATION ROAD

♿ P

1

EAST ST

WATERCRESS LINE

Winchester

B3046

0   ½ mile

0   500m

1. From the car park walk down Station Road to the T-junction with West Street. Turn right, then left down Broad Street and keep left at the bottom along Mill Hill. Halfway down, turn left into Ladywell Lane and soon after join the river bank and pass the attractive timbered and thatched Fulling Mill Cottage which straddles the River Arle.

2. Continue to the bottom of Dean Lane and turn right to keep to the riverside path. Cross a footbridge over the river at the redbrick Eel House, and ascend to pass a modern home, Drove House. Continue along a fenced path and then, on meeting the concrete driveway, turn right up it to the lane. Turn left at the lane and, as it bends left, fork right onto the Wayfarer's Walk and follow it to a junction of tracks. Bear right uphill to a lane beside Pinglestone Barn.

3. Turn left, descend to Fobdown Farm and take the road on the right beside the farm buildings. Follow the track ahead. On reaching a T-junction of tracks, turn left and keep to the track for 0.5 miles (800m) to a lane. Just before you reach the lane, the field on your left hides the site of the lost medieval village of Abbotstone, once a flourishing community with a manor, church and mill.

4. Bear right downhill, then right again along a track signed to Abbotstone Farmhouse. Keep ahead at the first junction, then ignore the waymarked track right (Wayfarer's Walk), and proceed ahead on the track which, in 0.5 miles (800m), descends to a lodge and the entrance to The Grange.

5. Turn left at Swarraton Lodge and follow the drive for 0.25 miles (400m) to visit this fine building, then retrace your steps, bearing left at Swarraton Lodge to the B3046. Turn right and immediately go through a kissing gate by the bus shelter into woodland. Continue through a second kissing gate then cross a driveway and follow the enclosed path left, beside the drive. Bear right alongside woodland to a tarmac drive. Cross straight over into woods to a road by a house. Turn left and left again before the gate to follow the footpath into Northfield Plantation. Keep ahead on the broad path, merging with a track.

6. Leave the wood and descend along the field-edge to a crossing of paths by a derelict barn. Proceed ahead following the telephone wires above to a gap in the hedge at the top of the field and follow the grassy path between fields.

7. Continue to beneath the telephone wires and pass a metal barn on the left, then after 75yds (70m) turn right onto a permissive path and walk along the field edge to a crossing of tracks. Turn left and follow the track for 0.5 miles (800m), gently descending into Old Alresford. Pass watercress beds on your right and follow the road right, beside the green, to reach the B3046.

8. Cross over and follow the pavement right to a lane opposite St Mary's church. Visit the church, cross the road and turn left to a grass triangle by a junction. Bear right along the lane, signed to Abbotstone and take the footpath ahead over a stream and beside watercress beds to Mill Hill and Broad Street.

Where to eat and drink

The Globe in New Alresford offers good pub food, decent ale and wine, and views across Old Alresford Pond from its waterside garden. Alternatively, try The Horse and Groom or, for good light lunches and teas, The Courtyard Tearooms off Broad Street.

TO DANEBURY HILL FROM STOCKBRIDGE

DISTANCE/TIME	7.7 miles (12.4km) / 3hrs 30min
ASCENT/GRADIENT	656ft (200m) / ▲
PATHS	Wide byways, field paths and railway track, 2 stiles
LANDSCAPE	Open downland and river valley
SUGGESTED MAP	OS Explorer 131 Romsey, Andover & Test Valley
START/FINISH	Grid reference: SU355351
DOG FRIENDLINESS	Can run free on Danebury Hill (prohibited in hill fort area)
PARKING	Along Stockbridge High Street
PUBLIC TOILETS	Danebury Hill (April to October) and on Stockbridge High Street

Stockbridge has developed from a frontier stronghold, built across the Test Valley by the Saxons to defend Wessex from marauding Danes, and a prosperous market town attracting Welsh sheep drovers en route to the markets in Surrey and Kent, to become Hampshire's 'fishing capital'. The clean waters of the River Test – one of England's finest chalk streams – are renowned for their trout fishing. On your journey down the long main street you will cross at least six branches of the Test, and a short diversion on to Common Marsh will give you rare access to the river bank. Much of the river bank in this area is reserved exclusively for wealthy fishing syndicates. The imposing 17th-century Grosvenor Hotel is the headquarters of the oldest and most select fishing club in the world, the Houghton Club, founded in 1822. Membership is limited to 24 and the club rigorously controls the fishing of the Test. The room above the distinctive overhanging porch, built so that coach travellers could alight under cover, is where the club's records have been kept since the club began.

Danish dock

Towards the end of your walk, as you cross the valley at Longstock, you will see one of the distinctive thatched fishing huts that are dotted along the banks of the river. Beside the hut, on a bridge across the river, you will notice some iron traps. Originally made from hazel, they were lowered into the river to catch eels. Behind the hut and hidden in the reeds are the remains of a 'Danish Dock', built to harbour flat-bottomed longboats. These may have belonged to King Canute, who sailed up the Test and destroyed Romsey. Before fishing for sport dominated village life, Stockbridge maintained its importance and wealth by becoming a horse-racing centre during the 19th century. Between 1753 and 1898, a racecourse existed high on the downs above the village and was a venue for important meetings in the racing calendar, on a par with Ascot and Goodwood. A frequent visitor was the Prince of Wales (later Edward VIII), who rented two properties in the village, one for himself and the other for his mistress Lillie Langtry. You can still see the old, ivy-covered stadium across the field below Chattis Hill as you make your way towards Danebury Hill. Your long and gradual climb out of the Test Valley culminates at an important Iron Age hill fort on top of Danebury Hill. This ancient earthwork covers 13 acres (5.2ha) and is a magnificent sight, with its double bank and ditch along with an inner rampart up to 16ft (5m) high in places. It was occupied by the Atrebates, a Celtic people, from about 550 to 100 BC and excavations have revealed a detailed picture of this Iron Age society. The far-reaching views across Hampshire and into Wiltshire from the fort's summit can take in six other hill forts on a clear day.

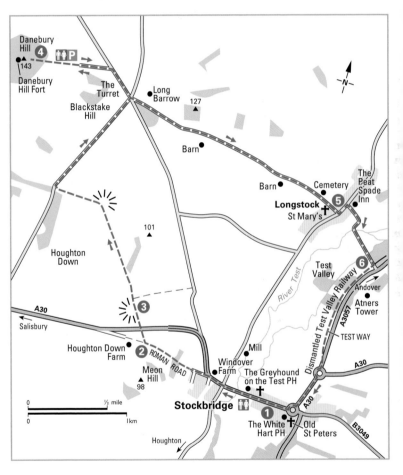

1. Walk west along the main street (A30), crossing the numerous braided streams of the River Test. Begin the climb out of the village and, just before the start of the dual carriageway, bear off to the left along Roman Road. Keep ahead at the end of the road, walking along the narrow defined path that climbs Meon Hill.

2. Just before Houghton Down Farm on your left, look out for a stile in the overgrown hedge on your right. Cross this and walk along the right-hand edge of a small orchard to a stile. Cross the A30 (with care), then walk through the narrow gap opposite and along the right-hand edge of a large field, keeping to the ditch, along the field boundary to your left.

3. Ignore the footpath turning on the right and keep to the main path, eventually bearing left with the field edge to a grassy track leading to a gate. Turn immediately right along a wide, hedged track and, when the track bends to the left into a field, keep ahead on a narrow grassy track to a road junction. To visit Danebury hill fort, turn left towards The Wallops for 400yds (366m), then left again along the drive to the car park and access to Danebury Hill.

4. Retrace your steps back to the road junction you passed before Danebury Hill and take the byway to the left beneath a height barrier. Remain on this track as it descends back into the Test Valley. Eventually it becomes metalled as it enters the village of Longstock.

5. At the T-junction by the church turn left then right beside The Peat Spade Inn, along 'The Bunny'. Cross numerous streams that make up the River Test, notably one with a thatched fishing hut and replica metal eel traps.

6. Just before crossing a bridge over the disused Test Valley railway and the A3057, take the narrow footpath on the right. Drop down and turn right along the old railway trackbed (here forming a part of the Test Way) for about a mile (1.6km). The path eventually merges with the pavement alongside the A3057, continue to reach the roundabout by The White Hart. Turn right here to return to your car.

Where to eat and drink

There's a good range of cafés and pubs in Stockbridge, notably The White Hart and The Greyhound on the Test. Imaginative food can be enjoyed at The Peat Spade Inn in Longstock.

What to see

A short distance along the Houghton road is the thatched Drovers' House. Dating from the 12th century, it was formerly an inn and provided lodgings for sheep drovers on their way from Wales to fairs in the South East. The inscription in Welsh reads 'seasoned hay, delicious pastures, good beer, comfortable beds'.

While you're there

Take the path by the side of Lillies of Stockbridge tearooms to access the 200 acres (81ha) known as Common Marsh. It was granted to the lords of the manor by charter some 900 years ago, allowing residents of Stockbridge to use it to graze their cattle – up to six beasts each. Now owned by the National Trust, it is one of the few places along the length of the Test that you can actually walk on the bank of the trout-filled river. Just to the south of Stockbridge you'll find Houghton Lodge Gardens overlooking the tranquil beauty of the River Test. Spacious lawns with fine trees surround the 18th-century fishing lodge and sweep down to the river.

KING'S SOMBORNE AND HORSEBRIDGE

DISTANCE/TIME	5.9 miles (9.5km) / 3hrs
ASCENT/GRADIENT	482ft (147m) / ▲ ▲
PATHS	Former railway track, field paths, tracks and road, 1 stile
LANDSCAPE	River valley, open farmland and downland
SUGGESTED MAP	OS Explorer 131 Romsey, Andover & Test Valley
START/FINISH	Grid reference: SU344304
DOG FRIENDLINESS	Off lead along the Test Way, otherwise keep under control
PARKING	Test Way car park at Horsebridge, opposite John O'Gaunt Inn
PUBLIC TOILETS	None en route

The tiny hamlet of Horsebridge is at the point where the original Roman road from Winchester to Old Sarum crossed the River Test. It is believed the Normans revived the old road to provide easy access from a hunting lodge, at Clarendon in Wiltshire, to a palace that probably existed at King's Somborne, and the huge deer park nearby. The proximity of the former deer park is reflected in the name of the pub, John O'Gaunt Inn, named after the prince who acquired the hunting ground following his marriage in 1359.

Hollows and bumps

King's Somborne takes its name from where the 'som' (swine) drank at or crossed the 'borne' (stream), with the royal connection dating back at least to Saxon times. In the *Domesday Book* of 1086, the manor was held by the Crown. Tradition has it that John of Gaunt (1340–99) had his palace behind the church in King's Somborne. Various hollows and humps in the field indicate the remains of a building, but excavations have only revealed evidence of an Anglo-Saxon settlement. There was a large manor house here in 1591 but 'John of Gaunt's Palace' is a more recent name based on the manor of King's Somborne being inherited by his wife in 1362. The Deer Park was created by William Briwere before 1200 and you can see parts of the 14th-century enclosing banks and yew trees as you leave the Test Valley and begin ascending on the Clarendon Way, and banks up to 10ft (3m) can be seen alongside the Horsebridge road. In the village you should also spy the village school next to the church. It was founded in 1842 by Reverend Richard Dawes and built from knapped flints salvaged from the ruins of the manor house. Your route follows the disused Test Valley Railway, or the 'Sprat and Winkle line' as it was affectionately known. It was built in 1865, replacing the canal that ran between Redbridge and Andover, but closed during the Beeching era in 1964. The Test Way, a long-distance path, follows it for 10 miles (16.1km) from Lower Brook to Fullerton.

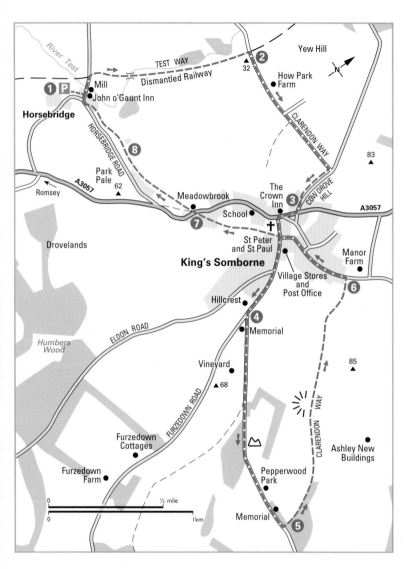

1. Leave the car park and turn left, opposite the John O'Gaunt Inn. Cross the River Test and turn right along the Test Way, dropping down on to the old railway line. After 0.75 miles (1.2km), pass beside a gate and turn right along the Clarendon Way.

2. Climb out of the valley, with the track becoming metalled at the top. Ignore turnings to the left and right, keeping straight ahead until, at the T-junction, you turn right with a waymarker down the left-hand edge of a field towards King's Somborne.

3. As you reach the houses in the field corner, descend the steps then turn right along the lane, and right again at the A3057 to enter the village. Turn left along Church Road opposite The Crown Inn. Ignore the lanes on the left and

right and gradually climb away from the village. Just past a house called Hillcrest, at the top of the hill, turn left at the fork, signed to Hoplands.

4. Follow this road past a memorial to footpath warden Mike Woodcock, and a vineyard on the right. Ignore the right of way to the right, and gently climb beside paddocks, following the road past Pepperwood Park. Keep ahead along a track and pass a memorial stone to four German airmen on your left.

5. Turn left along the Clarendon Way through a copse. Bear right and walk downhill on a narrow path beside paddocks and gallops, with splendid views across the Test Valley. Pass through a gap and follow the field edge ahead. Continue along the righthand edge of fields before descending to a lane in King's Somborne.

6. Turn left and walk through the village, following the lane left to a T-junction. Turn right and then left along a narrow footpath beside the churchyard wall. Besides an information board, enter an area of rough grassland. This is where John of Gaunt's palace is supposed to have been. Go ahead on a hard path to enter a playing field. Bear diagonally left across the field to the top left-hand corner. Go through a kissing gate to join a grassy path leading to a close of houses. Turn right then, before reaching the main road, turn left along a narrow fenced path between properties to the main road.

7. Cross straight over the A3057 and go through a kissing gate into pasture. Take the footpath slightly right across the field to its boundary and a kissing gate. Keep to the path that leads through gardens, via small gates, to a field.

8. Continue ahead towards a house and shortly cross the drive in front of it. Maintain your direction through further pasture to reach a stile and lane in Horsebridge. Turn right, then right again at the junction and turn left back into the Test Way car park.

Where to eat and drink
The Crown Inn in King's Somborne offers a homely atmosphere and good bar meals. Expect wholesome, home-made food at John O'Gaunt Inn, close to the Test Way at Horsebridge and popular with walkers (and dogs).

What to see
In the striking church of St Peter and St Paul in King's Somborne, note on the chancel floor two of England's oldest brasses, dated around 1380, which are thought to be of two of John of Gaunt's stewards. The war memorial in front of the church was designed by the famous architect Edwin Lutyens, who also designed Marsh Court, an elegant mansion overlooking the Test Valley near Stockbridge.

While you're there
The simple stone by Pepperwood Park remembers four German airmen who were shot down above Ashley Down in 1940 by Squadron Leader Bob Doe as their JU88 returned from a bombing raid on Manchester. After only seven days in action, he had already shot down four planes and this, his fifth, would make him an 'ace'. He thought it would be satisfying to see the wreckage, but he was sickened by it and vowed to never sightsee again.

WINCHESTER — ENGLAND'S ANCIENT CAPITAL

DISTANCE/TIME	5 miles (8.1km) / 2hrs 10mins
ASCENT/GRADIENT	302ft (92m) / ▲ ▲
PATHS	Established riverside paths through water-meadows
LANDSCAPE	City streets, riverside, water-meadow and downland
SUGGESTED MAP	OS Explorer OL32 Winchester, New Alresford & East Meon
START/FINISH	Grid reference: SU485294
DOG FRIENDLINESS	Keep under strict control
PARKING	Pay-and-display car parks in city centre
PUBLIC TOILETS	The Broadway; in cathedral visitor centre

Historic Winchester, ancient capital of Wessex and England, was first settled in the Iron Age. Influenced by royalty since the 7th century, the city boasts some remarkable architectural treasures.

Beginning from the imposing bronze statue of King Alfred the Great, who made the city his capital, this walk incorporates some of the famous sights, with a stroll through the water-meadows to the Hospital of St Cross, and St Catherine's Hill. From the Victorian Guildhall, you walk up the High Street, which has been a main thoroughfare to a crossing point on the River Itchen for some 2,500 years, before reaching the Cathedral Close. The magnificent cathedral was founded in 1079 on the site of an earlier Saxon building and remodelled in the 14th century. It is the longest medieval church in Europe and among its treasures are the 12th-century illuminated Winchester Bible, medieval wall paintings and the tombs of early English kings and more recent notables, including Jane Austen and Izaak Walton.

In the close you will find half-timbered Cheyney Court, formerly the Bishop's court house. Beyond Kingsgate you'll pass the entrance to the oldest school in England, Winchester College, founded in 1382 by William of Wykeham. Join a guided tour (in summer only) to view the handsome courtyards and cloisters, the chapel with its early 16th-century stained-glass window, and to savour the medieval atmosphere. At the end of College Street you'll see the Bishops of Winchester's house, the surviving wing of a grand palace built in 1684 overlooking the ruins of the 12th-century Wolvesey Castle.

Set in the wide, lush water-meadows beside the Itchen, at the end of the beautiful riverside walk beside the College grounds, is the Hospital of St Cross. Founded in 1132, it still functions as an almshouse and is the oldest charitable institution in the country. Here you can visit the fine Norman church, the Brethrens Hall and medieval kitchen, and take the 'Wayfarer's Dole' — bread and ale — a tradition that survives from the Middle Ages.

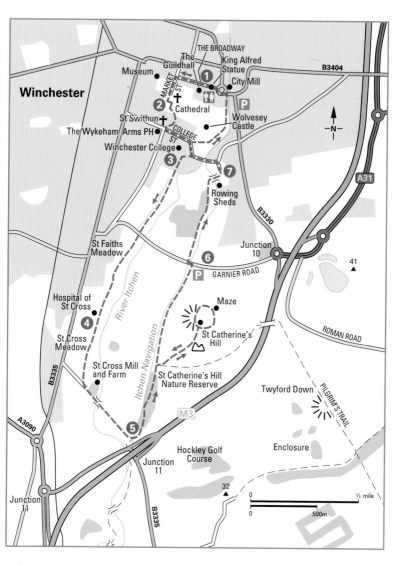

1. From King Alfred's statue on the Broadway, walk towards the city centre, passing the Guildhall (a tourist information centre) on your left. Join the High Street then, after 100yds (91m), turn left along Market Street. Continue ahead on to Cathedral Green to pass the cathedral's main door.

2. Turn left down a cloister (signed to Wolvesey Castle), then diagonally right through The Close to Cheyney Court and exit via Prior's Gate in the right-hand corner. Turn left though Kingsgate, with the tiny Church of St Swithun upon Kingsgate above, then turn left down College Street and soon after pass the entrance to Winchester College. Beyond the road barrier, turn right along College Walk, then turn right at the end of the wall, to walk along a college access road.

3. Go left by a gated entrance to the college. Follow the path beside the River Itchen for 0.5 miles (800m) to a road. Turn right over the road bridge and follow the riverside gravel path, signed the Clarendon Way, to a kissing gate. Cross a footbridge and head towards the Hospital of St Cross.

4. Keep left alongside the wall, go through a second kissing gate and walk ahead through an avenue of trees to a third kissing gate. Keep ahead on the path to two further kissing gates and join a farm track leading ahead to a traffic-free lane. Turn left and pass beside a barrier onto another traffic-free section and continue across the River Itchen and through a gate to reach a junction of metalled paths by the M3.

5. Turn left along a path, signed 'Itchen Navigation'. Go under an old railway bridge and pass through woodland. Go through a gate on your right and up the steps to the top of St Catherine's Hill, and walk around the top to see the maze and enjoy the fine views. Return to the bottom, turn right and almost immediately left to drop down to follow a narrow path by the Itchen Navigation. Go past the car park to the road.

6. Turn left across the bridge and take the footpath immediately right down through a kissing gate. Pass a memorial to the last river barge of 1869. Keep to the path beside the water, disregarding the path left (College nature reserve). Go through four kissing gates. Soon after, cross the brick Wharf Bridge by some rowing sheds to reach a metalled track.

7. Turn left, then left again at the road. Follow it along College Walk and turn right at the end onto a metalled path, alongside a high stone wall. Pass the Old Bishop's Palace (Wolvesey Castle) and follow the path beside the Itchen to Bridge Street, opposite the National Trust's City Mill. Finally, turn left to return to King Alfred's statue.

Where to eat and drink
Old pubs, tearooms and restaurants abound near the cathedral and its close. Try the excellent Cathedral Refectory, the eighteen71 café behind the Guildhall or The Wykeham Arms in Kingsgate Street.

What to see
St Catherine's Hill, Winchester's most prominent natural landmark, is well worth the detour as you head back into the city. It was the site of the area's first settlement and on its summit are the rampart and ditch of an Iron Age hill fort, the Norman remains of St Catherine's Chapel, and a 17th-century turf-cut maze. You'll also be rewarded with excellent views of the city.

While you're there
Allow time to visit Winchester's City Museum on the edge of the Cathedral Green. It tells the story of the city, as an important Roman town and the principal city of King Alfred, through Anglo-Saxon and Norman England to modern times.

TICHBORNE AND THE WAYFARER'S WALK

DISTANCE/TIME	5.8 miles (9.4km) / 2hrs 45min
ASCENT/GRADIENT	486ft (148m) / ▲
PATHS	Field paths, downland tracks and some road walking, 6 stiles
LANDSCAPE	River valley and undulating farmland dotted with woodland
SUGGESTED MAP	OS Explorer OL32 Winchester, New Alresford & East Meon
START/FINISH	Grid reference: SU583286
DOG FRIENDLINESS	Keep dogs under control
PARKING	Cheriton. Roadside parking on village lane east of B3046
PUBLIC TOILETS	None on route

Tiny Tichborne is idyllic. Thatched and timber-framed cottages line the lane that winds up to St Andrew's Church, handsome farms and the magnificent manor house nestle close to the infant River Itchen. This gentle ramble incorporates two of Hampshire's long-distance trails, the Itchen Way and the Wayfarer's Walk, on its way to the unspoilt and intriguing estate village.

Oldest seat

The manor has been the seat of the Tichbornes since 1135, although the present building dates from 1803. The Tichborne Dole is one of the oldest surviving traditions in Britain. It's said that, in the 13th century, Lady Mabella Tichborne, wife of Sir Roger Tichborne, decided on her deathbed to provide a 'dole' of bread for the poor of the parish on Lady Day, 25 March. Sir Roger, who was not a charitable man, reluctantly granted her request for a piece of land to ensure that the dole would continue after her death, on one condition. She could have as much land as she could get around unaided, while a firebrand stayed alight. Although weak and unable to walk, she managed to crawl around 23 acres (9.3ha) of land which is still known as 'The Crawls'. To this day every parishioner of Tichborne and Cheriton receives a gallon of flour when they assemble at Tichborne House on Lady Day.

The Tichborne family was also involved in the controversy of the Tichborne Claimant. Another Roger Tichborne was presumed lost at sea in 1854, but his mother placed adverts in the press offering a reward for the discovery of her missing son. In 1872, a man arrived from Australia claiming to be her son. Even at 24 stone (152kg) and in middle age (Roger was younger and slim), he convinced the mother that he was her son and they swore affidavits before she died. The family contested his claim to the family fortune and the ensuing Tichborne Claimant case lasted ten months. Eventually Arthur Orton, a Wapping butcher, was jailed for 14 years but the action cost the family £80,000.

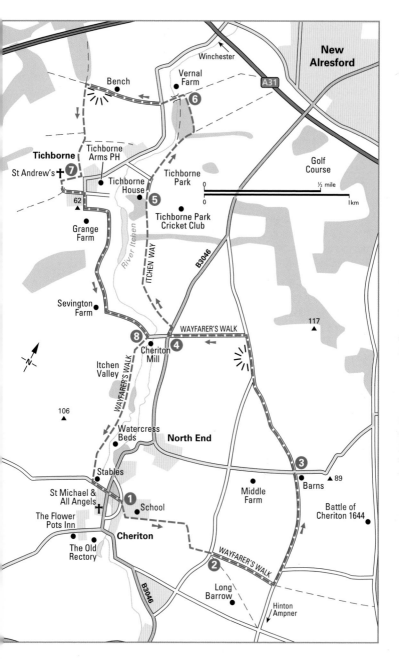

1. From the village lane, cross the small brick bridge opposite Old Kennetts Cottage and bear right in front of the school. Just beyond a house (Martyrwell), turn left along a narrow fenced path (signed Wayfarers Walk) and climb out of the village. Turn right and then left around the field edge to a stile and crossing of paths.

2. Proceed straight ahead along the grassy track to a crossing of routes. Turn left downhill. The fields to your right were the site of the Battle of Cheriton in 1644. Keep to the track to a lane beside a pair of barns.

3. Cross the lane and walk along the farm track. A track merges from the left, beyond which you climb to a junction of paths. Enjoying lovely views across the Itchen Valley, turn left downhill, following the track to the B3046, heading towards a cluster of buildings.

4. Turn right and, after 70yds (64m), cross the road and take the path left, across the field and at the field boundary turn slightly right across the second field, parallel with the river, to a narrow belt of trees. Walk through the trees, cross the stile and keep to the left-hand edge of pasture (Tichborne House is to the left) to a stile by the drive entrance.

5. Turn right and keep ahead, then, where the metalled estate road curves left, proceed along a track. Just before you reach some woodland, bear off right along a grassy track through a line of trees into a field. Take the permissive path left along the field edge.

6. Turn left onto the lane, pass Vernal Farm, then cross the infant River Itchen to a lane. Take the path opposite, uphill along the field edge. In the top left-hand corner, passing a bench, follow the track left into a second field. Turn left along the field edge, downhill towards St Andrew's church. Ignore tracks right and left and continue to the village (The Tichborne Arms is to the left).

7. Just before the road, take the path right uphill to the church. On leaving the church, follow the access lane downhill to a T-junction. Turn right and follow the quiet road for a mile (1.6km), close to Tichborne Park and the river, to Cheriton Mill.

8. Follow the Wayfarer's Walk right, beside the mill to a gate. Walk in front of a neat cottage to a kissing gate and continue ahead, parallel with the river. Go through two gates very close together and maintain your direction over stiles by gates. Continue to an angled gap in the fence and turn left along the lane to the B3046 in Cheriton. Cross over to reach the village lane and your car.

Where to eat and drink

The thatched Tichborne Arms offers home-made food, real ale and a garden – dogs are welcome. In Cheriton, post-walk refreshment can be enjoyed at The Flower Pots Inn, noted for its home-brewed beers, bar food and warm welcome.

What to see

Have a look inside St Andrew's church at Tichborne, which dates back to the 11th century. As well as some rather splendid box pews from the 17th century, it has some less obvious and much more recent additions. The glass windows on either side of the main door were created as a millenium project. They depict local agricultural scenes, and mark church festivals in the farming year: Plough, Rogation, Lammas and Harvest.

HAWKLEY
TO STEEP

DISTANCE/TIME	7.5 miles (12km) / 4hrs 30min
ASCENT/GRADIENT	1,611ft (491m) / ▲ ▲ ▲
PATHS	Field and woodland paths, rutted, wet and muddy tracks and short stretches of road, 11 stiles
LANDSCAPE	Rolling, beech-clad hills, a hidden, flower-filled valley and undulating farmland
SUGGESTED MAP	OS Explorer OL33 Haslemere & Petersfield
START/FINISH	Grid reference: SU746291
DOG FRIENDLINESS	Dogs to be kept under control at all times
PARKING	By village green and church in Hawkley
PUBLIC TOILETS	None; outdoor toilets opposite Harrow Inn accessible
NOTES	Several steep climbs make this walk very challenging – but the views make the challenges worthwhile.

William Cobbett wrote 'beautiful beyond description' in his *Rural Rides*, after passing through Hawkley in 1822, on his way from East Meon to Thursley. Cobbett was enchanted by the rolling, beech-clad hills that characterise this relatively unexplored part of Hampshire.

Abiding love

Known locally as 'hangers', from the Anglo-Saxon *hangra*, meaning 'sloping wood', these fine beech woods cling to the steep chalk escarpment that links Selborne to Steep. Many have charming names such as Happersnapper Hanger and Strawberry Hanger. Edward Thomas lived at Steep from 1906 to his death in 1917, and his first home here was Berryfield. His abiding love for the beech hangers, mysterious combes and the sheer beauty of the landscape inspired him to write some of his finest poems, including 'Up in the Wind', 'The New House' and 'Wind and Mist'. You, too, will find the views breathtaking as you dip and climb through the hangers to the summit of Shoulder of Mutton Hill, Thomas's favoured spot above his beloved Steep.

The walk begins from Hawkley, tucked away beneath Hawkley Hanger. You descend into the lush meadows of the Oakshott Valley, before a steep ascent on an old droving track to the top of Shoulder of Mutton Hill. Here, in a tranquil glade on its higher slopes, you will find a sarsen stone dedicated to Edward Thomas. With views across Steep and of 'sixty miles of South Downs at one glance', as Thomas described it, it is no wonder that he loved this area. The return walk joins the Hangers Way, a 21-mile (33.8km) long-distance trail traversing East Hampshire from Queen Elizabeth Country Park to Alton.

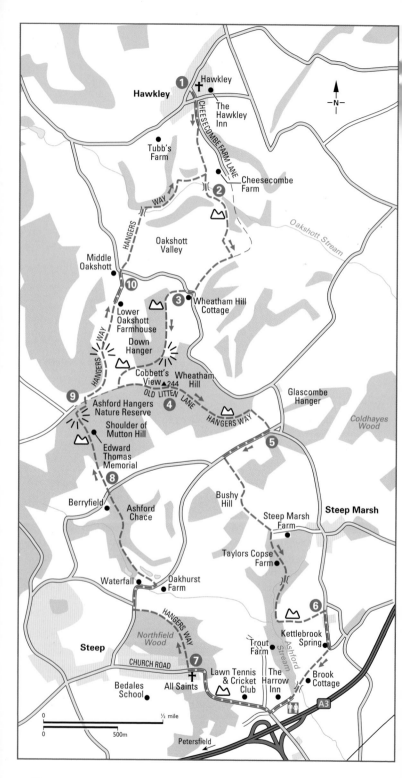

1. With your back to Hawkley church, walk left beside the green to the road junction. With The Hawkley Inn away to your left, cross over down Cheesecombe Farm Lane. Shortly, bear right along a concrete path, signed 'Hangers Way', and soon after bear left onto path. Descend to cross a stile and keep straight on at the fork of paths, hugging the left edge of the field with Cheesecombe Farm to the left.

2. Cross a stile and bridge over Oakshott stream and then another stile and keep left along the field edge beside woodland. Steeply ascend to cross a stile, and follow the fenced path uphill and left. Drop down to a track and turn right, to reach a junction, then right again for 55yds (50m) to take the waymarked track straight ahead.

3. Climb the long and steep chalky track up through Down Hanger (this can get very wet and muddy), with views east along the South Downs unfolding. At the top of Wheatham Hill, turn left, with a sign for Ashford Hangers National Nature Reserve ahead. Pass a barrier and follow the gravel track.

4. Turn left up the second set of steps to enjoy Cobbett's View. Return to the main track and continue downhill for 0.5 miles (800m). Just before a gate and a lane, climb the stile right and descend through an avenue of trees and across a field to a stile and lane. Turn right.

5. After 400yds (366m), take the footpath left, to the left of a gate. Descend to a metal kissing gate and bear gently right across the field to another kissing gate by a telegraph pole. Turn left over a stile and follow the field edge via another stile to Steep Marsh Farm. Turn right across the ends of the large barns and join a wooded track. Keep left at a junction of paths. Shortly after, cross the drive to Taylors Copse Farm and back into woodland. Cross a stream. Just before a curving drive, climb the short steep path left within the trees to a stile. Follow the signed path across the field ahead to a stile, and continue onto a track by stables, pass the stables on your left and reach a lane.

6. Turn right, passing three houses, then, at a sharp left bend, bear off right into woodland. Walk above a small ravine and past a pair of timbered cottages to a footbridge. Continue ahead and pass The Harrow Inn. Turn right at the junction and walk uphill into Steep to All Saints church.

7. Follow the Hangers Way opposite, across a playing field and down through Northfield Wood to a kissing gate. Walk along the left-hand field edge to a kissing gate and road. Turn right and then, as it swings right, keep ahead up the footpath (the waterfall is to your left). At a junction, turn left and walk through light woodland. Emerge onto a drive just by the gates to The Waterhouse, and turn right leading up to a lane beside Ashford Chace.

8. Turn right and then almost immediately left along a footpath towards Shoulder of Mutton Hill. Enter the Ashford Hangers National Nature Reserve and immediately take the middle of three paths ahead to climb steeply up the grassy scarp slope to the Edward Thomas memorial stone. At the top, go through a barrier and keep straight ahead to reach a track. Turn right beside the Ashford Hangers NNR sign, then after 200yds (183m) bear left up a path into the woodland. On reaching a crosstrack head straight across through a kissing gate.

9. Follow the Hangers Way as it descends through three kissing gates, through the edge of beech woods and steeply down across meadowland, through

another kissing gate to a path between fields, eventually joining the drive to Lower Oakshott Farmhouse and a road.

10. Turn right then left through the gap and follow the defined Hangers Way path through the Oakshott Valley, crossing stiles, plank bridges and delightful meadows to reach the junction of paths before Cheesecombe Farm. Turn left to the stile. Retrace your steps back to Hawkley and your car.

Where to eat and drink

Time your walk to coincide with lunch at the delightfully unspoilt 16th-century Harrow Inn at Steep (credit cards not accepted). There are two characterful rooms with scrubbed wooden tables and warming winter fires. Expect ale straight from the cask, hearty soup and sandwiches, and a cottage garden for summer imbibing. No children at the bar. The equally rustic Hawkley Inn offers a warm welcome to walkers, microbrewery ales and imaginative home-cooked food.

What to see

In Steep, the partly Norman church contains a memorial window to Edward Thomas etched by Lawrence Whistler (1912—2000). The church lies close to Bedales School, which first attracted the poet to the village in 1906, so that his children could attend the school.

While you're there

Track down the White Horse, at grid reference SU 714289, just off on the unclassified road from Petersfield to the A32. Known locally as 'the pub with no name', it's a classic example of an unspoilt country pub and was a regular haunt of Edward Thomas — his tankard still hangs in the bar. The pub inspired his first poem 'Up in the Wind' (1914), which describes the inn's isolation. It begins: 'I could wring the old thing's neck that put it there! A public-house'.

A WEST MEON VALLEY RAMBLE

DISTANCE/TIME	3.5 miles (5.7km) / 1hr 30min
ASCENT/GRADIENT	449ft (137m) / ▲ ▲
PATHS	Country tracks, minor roads and field paths
LANDSCAPE	Rolling arable farmland with a few trees
SUGGESTED MAP	OS Explorer OL32 Winchester New Alresford & East Meon
START/FINISH	Grid reference: SU642236
DOG FRIENDLINESS	Keep under close control; lead required for crossing the A32
PARKING	Meon Valley Trail car park
PUBLIC TOILETS	None on route

More than half a century after the last public trains steamed along the Meon Valley Railway, begin your walk just off Station Road in West Meon's former goods yard. It's now a car park for the popular 10-mile (16.1km) railway walk south to Wickham but there's still plenty to see here. The overgrown platforms stretch beneath the road bridge and if you've a head for heights you can walk along the towering embankment to the start of the demolished viaduct.

A railway failure

The railway is an extraordinary tale of commercial rivalry and defeat snatched from the jaws of victory. By the end of the 19th century, the powerful London and South Western Railway was the dominant player in Hampshire and southern England. Its lines had already penetrated as far west as Padstow on the north Cornish coast — deep into the territory of its main competitor, the Great Western. For its part, the Great Western had driven south from Reading to Basingstoke and from Didcot to Winchester and now had the Portsmouth and south coast traffic firmly in its sights.

The London and South Western was having none of it. The company successfully promoted its own line south from Basingstoke, continuing down the Meon Valley to Fareham and effectively frustrating the Great Western's ambitions. The company spared no expense in laying out its new route with lavish stations, smooth curves and easy gradients designed to accommodate double track. Nevertheless, it started life in 1903 as a single track railway, with passing loops at the intermediate stations.

But it was to prove a hollow victory. With its heavy earthworks and tunnels, the Meon Valley line was expensive to maintain and the traffic in this thinly populated area simply didn't materialise. The railway was never upgraded to double track; services were progressively cut back and changes in the 1930s further downgraded the route's status and passenger appeal. The line couldn't compete in the harsh economic climate that followed World War II and all services were withdrawn in 1955.

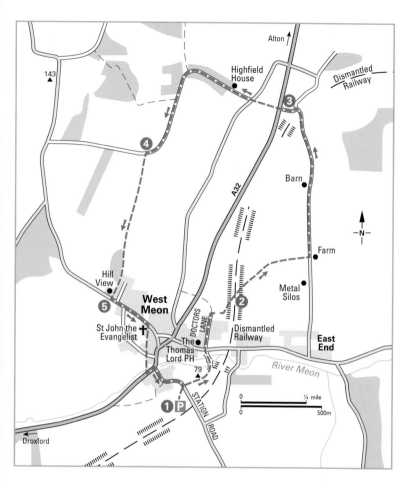

1. From the car park, walk back down the station approach, cross Station Road and take the signposted footpath opposite running between two low brick walls. Keep left. Cross two footbridges, then turn left along the village road for 60yds (55m) before turning right up Doctors Lane. Walk between the gateposts at The Cedars, keep ahead to a field and, just before reaching it, fork right at the signpost, follow the overgrown path to a kissing gate and bear right across a paddock to a second kissing gate.

2. Walk up steps to cross the old railway and walk diagonally across the field to a gap in the far left-hand corner. Bear right, continue under power lines and cross the next field to reach a tarmac lane by farm buildings. Turn left, continue over the hill and drop down across the old railway bridge, then bear left and up to the A32.

3. Take great care as you cross the main road and keep ahead up the sunken track opposite. Cross a metalled lane, continue along the signposted bridleway and keep ahead past Highfield House. Now follow the track as it curves left, and stay on the main track for a quarter of a mile (400m). Stay with the main track as it bears right, left and right again.

4. Where it goes sharp right, turn left at a waymarked barrier in the hedge and follow the grassy track down through the shallow valley to reach the road at Hill View.

5. Turn left past Long Priors, keep ahead over the low summit and turn right into the churchyard. Turn left at the church porch, follow the path out of the churchyard gate on the left and keep ahead over the driveway to the A32. Cross over with care, zig-zag left and right into Station Road and continue up the station approach to the car park.

Where to eat and drink

The Thomas Lord in West Meon is a smart dining pub which favours local, seasonal produce. A range of tasty sandwiches and lighter meals are available at lunchtime.

What to see

Turn right briefly when you reach the River Meon near the start of your walk to see the massive concrete foundations of the former railway viaduct. The engineers had originally planned a conventional arched crossing of the valley, but the soft ground forced them to extend the embankments and erect a 62ft (19m) high steel viaduct instead.

While you're there

Take a look around West Meon's church, St John the Evangelist. Sir George Gilbert Scott's pleasing Gothic Revival building was consecrated in 1846. Thomas Lord, the founder of Lord's Cricket Ground, is buried in the churchyard.

MEANDERING AROUND MOTTISFONT

22

DISTANCE/TIME	4.2 miles (6.8km) / 2hrs
ASCENT/GRADIENT	279ft (85m) / ▲
PATHS	Easy woodland trails and field paths, 2 stiles
LANDSCAPE	Water-meadows, farmland and National Trust woodland
SUGGESTED MAP	OS Explorer 131 Romsey, Andover & Test Valley
START/FINISH	Grid reference: SU315277
DOG FRIENDLINESS	Can be let off lead in Spearywell Wood; allowed in Mottisfont gardens but not the Walled Garden
PARKING	National Trust car park at Spearywell Wood
PUBLIC TOILETS	In abbey gardens (only if visiting abbey)

This short walk explores the National Trust estate at Mottisfont. Set picturesquely beside the River Test and around the walls of a former 12th-century priory, Mottisfont is a charming village of thatched cottages and Georgian houses, complete with a splendid listed church and an old tithe barn. The village's name is derived from 'moot's font' or 'spring of the meeting place', which rises in a deep pool in the abbey grounds.

Whether you start the walk from Mottisfont Abbey car park (seasonal opening) or from Spearywell Wood, you will find strolling through the village a real delight. Beginning from the latter, the walk explores good estate paths through woodland, then gradually descends into the Dun Valley, offering you serene views west across rolling downland into fertile Wiltshire.

The abbey and St Andrew's

Originally an Augustinian priory church, founded by William Briwere in 1201, Mottisfont Abbey never actually achieved the full status of an abbey and struggled to survive until the Dissolution of the Monasteries. Between 1536 and 1540 it was owned by William, Lord Sandys, who converted the buildings into a mansion. It was during the 18th century that much of the medieval cloisters were destroyed and the romantic title 'abbey' given to the building. Although the buildings are mainly private, you can still see some medieval arches, the 13th-century monks' cellarium and a masterpiece of trompe-l'oeil work by Rex Whistler, one of the great British artists of the 20th century, in the Drawing Room. You will find the sweeping lawns and mature trees which run down to the River Test very peaceful and well worth spending a few quiet moments enjoying.

You should not miss St Andrew's church in Mottisfont. Dating from the 12th century and Grade 1 listed, it contains more 15th-century stained glass that any other Hampshire church, a fine Norman chancel and a rare clock mechanism from about 1620 – the only other one in working order is in Salisbury Cathedral.

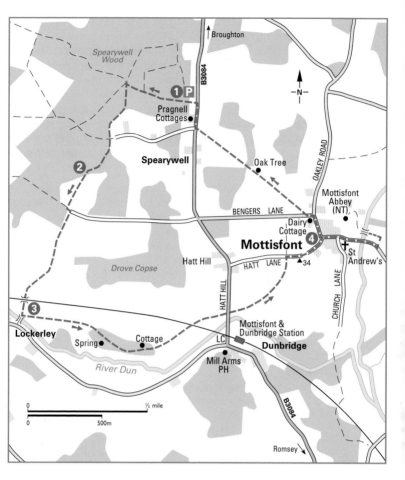

1. Pass beside the gate opposite the Spearywell Wood car park entrance, by the information boards, to join a woodland path. Follow the white arrows as it bears right, and pass through a tall conifer plantation; then, where the path reaches a T-junction, turn left (by a concrete marker stone indicating a Mottisfont Estate Path, MEP). Bear right at the next junction (MEP stone), then at the staggered junction by a red spot waymarker, bear left then immediately right through woodland. Descend through the woodland fringe and at a fork keep right, following a yellow waymarker to a junction.

2. Turn left across a plank bridge and then diagonally right across a field. At a gap in the hedge and crossing of paths, zig-zag right (MEP stone) then left, following an estate path along the woodland edge and past a redundant stile Continue beside fencing, eventually passing under the railway to a footbridge over the River Dun. The Dun, a tributary of the Test, was also known as the Barge River. At one time there were plans to develop a new canal to link Southampton and Salisbury, but the scheme was never completed.

3. Don't cross the river. Turn left through the kissing gate (MEP stone) and follow the path across meadow and rough, marshy pasture, keeping the

telegraph poles on your right, crossing two plank bridges to a stile at the end by the oak trees. Bear right through a gate and follow the fence on your left. Continue through a copse, passing a spring then an isolated thatched cottage to a kissing gate by a gate. Proceed along the driveway and when it bends right by a lone oak (MEP stone) bear left, on a grassy track towards the railway. Cross the line (take great care; look and listen), then follow the track to a gate and the B3084. Turn right if you wish to visit the Mill Arms at Dunbridge. Otherwise, cross over to join a path signed to 'Mottisfont Abbey and Village Centre', proceeding slightly left up the slope and through a kissing gate. In the next field cross to the trees and follow the path to reach a narrow tarmac lane, and turn right.

4. At the T-junction, turn right for the entrance to Mottisfont Abbey. Retrace your steps along the road and follow it as it bears right to a junction, opposite the old abbey gates. Turn left along Bengers Lane and take the path right, diagonally across the field towards a lone oak tree. Go through a belt of trees and proceed through the next field to a gate. Turn right along the road for 150yds (137m) to return to the car park.

Where to eat and drink
The abbey has its own restaurant and café. A short diversion from your walk, just beyond half way, will lead you to the Mill Arms at Dunbridge for well-presented food, decent ales and a pleasant summer garden.

What to see
While strolling the magnificent grounds surrounding Mottisfont Abbey, look out for the old Ice House behind the stables. Few remain in the county in such good condition.

While you're there
If you're here in June, make sure you see the national collection of old-fashioned (pre-1900) roses, planted in the walled kitchen garden of the abbey in 1972. The colour and heady perfume of thousands of roses on a balmy June evening is a magical experience.

ROMSEY AND ITS ABBEY

DISTANCE/TIME	5.9 miles (9.5km) / 2hrs 30min
ASCENT/GRADIENT	207ft (63m) / ▲
PATHS	Towpath, field and muddy woodland paths, some roads, 4 stiles
LANDSCAPE	Initially urban, followed by water-meadows, rolling farmland and dense woodland
SUGGESTED MAP	OS Explorer 131 Romsey, Andover & Test Valley
START/FINISH	Grid reference: SU352211
DOG FRIENDLINESS	Some road walking; keep under strict control in conservation areas
PARKING	Pay-and-display car parks in Romsey town centre
PUBLIC TOILETS	By Romsey bus station

Romsey is the best preserved of all Hampshire's market towns. Located beside the beautiful River Test, it developed around a Benedictine nunnery founded in AD 907 by Edward the Elder, son of Alfred the Great, whose daughter, Aelfreda, became the first abbess. By the end of the 10th century there was a small town outside the perimeter walls of the abbey, whose inhabitants served the needs of the growing community of nuns. Much of the great abbey church you see today was built between 1120 and 1130 by Henry de Blois, Bishop of Winchester, but traces of the earlier Saxon church can be seen, notably two beautifully carved rood sculptures dating from AD 1000. The abbey is now recognised as one of Europe's most impressive Norman churches, and is certainly the finest in Hampshire.

An abbey in name only

The magnificent abbey was saved from destruction at the Dissolution, although the surrounding convent buildings were not so lucky. In 1544 the town secured an agreement with Henry VIII and bought the abbey and its surrounding land for £100. You can see a copy of the bill of sale, signed and sealed by Henry VIII, in the south choir aisle. How the money was raised is still one of Romsey's great mysteries as no records have been found. You can marvel at the scale and splendour of the architecture, notably the massive pillars and rounded arches, view medieval paintings and tapestries, and seek out the monuments to Lord Palmerston, a Victorian Conservative prime minister, Sir William Petty, economist and founder of the Royal Society, and Earl Mountbatten.

Against the backdrop of the abbey you will find splendid Georgian houses tucked away on winding side streets reflecting Romsey's days as a thriving brewing and market town. Opposite the abbey stands King John's House (1240), one of England's oldest surviving dwellings. The walk leaves town by the only surviving stretch of the Andover and Redbridge Canal. Completed in 1794, it was 22 miles (35.4km) long and rose 164ft (50m) via 24 locks. It was never a real success and the arrival of the railway forced its closure in 1857. The towpath takes you into the Test Valley and you will soon be walking beside the clear waters of Hampshire's most famous chalk stream. Beyond The Duke's Head, a gentle climb through Squabb Wood leads you back to the water-meadows close to the Test and the restored Sadler's Mill.

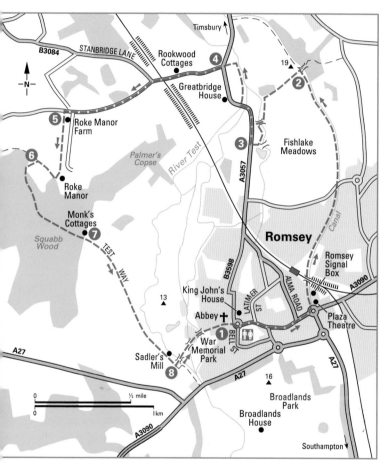

1. From the Market Square head east along The Hundred, passing the police station, and continue into Winchester Road. At the roundabout, turn left just before the Plaza Theatre to join a footpath to Cupernham and Timsbury. Walk alongside the old canal as it passes under the railway and then a road bridge, and leave town into open meadowland.

2. At a crossing of paths (with a bridge to the right and soon after the canal widens), turn left and walk across the meadows on a gravel path. Bear right across a bridge onto a dirt path until you reach the River Test. Turn left along the riverbank, cross a bridge and walk along the opposite bank to a block driveway by a house. Turn right along the drive to the A3057 and turn right.

3. Follow the pavement and cross the River Test, then take the footpath immediately right alongside the river. Pass a bridge, then follow the official diversion left around a house to a track. Turn left to the main road.

4. Cross the road to join the B3084, signed to Roke Manor. Carefully walk along this busy road (there are some verges) for 0.5 miles (800m), then just beyond the railway bridge fork left for Roke Manor. Pass the entrance to the manor and take the drive on the left signed to Roke Manor Farm.

5. Pass Roke Manor Farm then, on nearing offices by the manor, bear right along the road for 60yds (55m). Take the footpath right, signed 'To the Test Way' (it can be overgrown) and shortly bear right through a hedge, then left between fields. Go ahead into the copse and turn left to locate a Test Way sign.

6. Walk through Squabb Wood on a bracken-lined path and cross a plank bridge to reach a junction of paths. Keep left with the Test Way and go through the wood, via three plank bridges and a stile, looking for the Test Way markers.

7. Leave the wood at a bridge with a stile at either end, and bear slightly right across the field to two gates and a footbridge, then bear slightly left to further stiles and a footbridge, heading towards farm buildings. Keep to the left-hand edge of the field, pass through two kissing gates and follow the track as it bears left between houses to the River Test by Sadler's Mill.

8. Bear left at the mill and leave the Test Way. Cross the river, follow a tarmac path and soon pass the War Memorial Park. Continue along a road close to the abbey back into the Market Square.

Where to eat and drink
There are plenty of pubs, restaurants and cafés in Romsey, notably Miss Moody's Tudor Tea Room at King John's House, the Olive Tree, the Courtyard Coffee House, and the excellent Three Tuns.

What to see
If you are visiting King John's House (off Church Street), look for the small exposed section of knuckle-bone floor, made from cattle bones in the 17th century, and the graffiti scratched by daggers on the plaster walls in 1306. In the autumn, at Sadler's Mill on the Test, look out for salmon leaping the weir as they return to their spawning grounds.

While you're there
Visit Broadlands, the home of Lord Mountbatten. This elegant Palladian mansion enjoys a lovely setting by the River Test and you can view inside the house during limited times of the year.

THE MEON VALLEY NATURE RESERVE

DISTANCE/TIME	7 miles (11.3km) / 3hrs 30min
ASCENT/GRADIENT	889ft (271m) / ▲▲
PATHS	Field paths, footpaths, tracks and sections of road, 7 stiles
LANDSCAPE	Chalk downland, gently rolling farmland and river valley
SUGGESTED MAP	OS Explorer OL3 Meon Valley, Portsmouth, Gosport & Fareham
START/FINISH	Grid reference: SU645214
DOG FRIENDLINESS	Lead required through villages and around nature reserve
PARKING	Natural England car park off Old Winchester Hill Lane
PUBLIC TOILETS	None on route

Old Winchester Hill dominates the Meon Valley. From its summit, some 648ft (197m) above sea level, are far-reaching views across the Solent to the Isle of Wight, west to the New Forest and Wiltshire, and north to Beacon Hill. It's long been a natural vantage point, attracting early settlers who preferred the safety of the high ground. The remains of the fort on the summit date back to the Iron Age. Its defences comprise a massive single bank and ditch enclosing about 14 acres (5.6ha). The oval-shaped fort overlies a pattern of prehistoric fields and you will notice some large grassy mounds as you walk round the rampart. These are Bronze Age burial mounds, erected on the crest of the hill between 4,500 and 3,500 years ago for important members of society.

Nature reserve

Old Winchester Hill was purchased by the state in 1954 and is now a National Nature Reserve, cared for by Natural England. The sheep-grazed chalk downland, with its mix of open grassland, scrub and woodland, is home to a number of rare butterflies and chalk-loving flowers. Walk this way in early summer and you will see the hill fort dotted with fragrant orchids, while in July look out for the bright blue round-headed rampion, a rarity in Britain, which thrives here. On a warm August day the grassland is a sea of colour with hundreds of plants, flowers and wild herbs. An area just 1m (3ft) square can contain 30 to 40 different species of plant and over 200 species have been recorded on the reserve. Chalkhill blue butterflies feed on the wild majoram, the plants on the reserve providing food for some 34 species of butterfly and their caterpillars. The longer grass is favoured by hedge and meadow browns and the beautiful marbled white butterflies. You may see a peregrine falcon hunting, buzzards soaring high on the thermals, and summer migrants like the redstart and pied flycatcher. In winter, fieldfares and redwings feed on juniper berries, while the yew woods provide shelter to titmice and goldcrests.

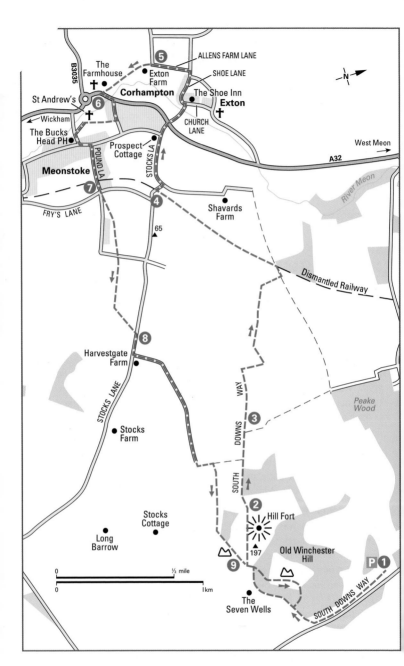

1. From the car park go through the gate onto the open downland and turn left, leaving the information board on your right. Follow the path around the perimeter of the reserve, merge with the South Downs Way (SDW) and bear right towards the hill fort. Go straight through a gate then bear left, then right, across the centre of the fort.

2. Descend through the ramparts, downhill to a kissing gate on the edge of woodland. Pass beneath yew trees and beside a redundant gate, then along a field, and when the path swings right at a fingerpost, go left onto the SDW.

3. Follow the enclosed path downhill to reach a junction of paths. Cross the footbridge and turn left, following the signposted 'SDW'. Climb the steps on to the former Meon Valley railway, and turn left along the old line for just over half a mile (800m).

4. Turn left at a gate and drop down to a lane, turn right under the missing bridge, then immediately left at the junction. Walk along Stocks Lane to the A32 and carefully cross the main road into Beacon Hill Lane, and over the river. Turn left just before The Shoe Inn, and shortly after bear left along Allens Farm Lane.

5. At a sharp right-hand bend, keep ahead along the path beside Exton Farm. Go through two gates on a fenced path then through a small field to a kissing gate and then another fenced path to a stile. Pass beside The Farmhouse, the White House and the church, bearing left to the A32.

6. Carefully cross the A32, turn left along the pavement and right by the shop. Take the metalled path beside the last house on your right and enter Meonstoke churchyard. Turn left along the lane to a T-junction beside The Bucks Head. Turn left, then left again at the junction. Follow the lane right (Pound Lane) to cross the old railway and reach a crossroads.

7. Climb the stile on your left. Go across the field and cross a stile to pass behind gardens, eventually reaching a stile and crossing a lane. Climb the stile opposite and keep to the right-hand field edge to cross another stile. At the next stile, bear diagonally left towards a house, Harvestgate, and road.

8. Turn right and take the track left just before Harvestgate Farm. Keep ahead through a gate. At the top of the track, bear left uphill along the field edge, then sharp right onto SDW, following the bridleway along the hedge and into the next field. Turn through a kissing gate on your left into the nature reserve and ascend steeply to the hill fort ramparts.

9. Bear right and then right again to join the outward route by the fort entrance. Turn left to walk down the steps beside a seat and information board, and then continue to follow a path just beneath the downland rim. Bear right to a kissing gate and retrace your steps to the car park.

Where to eat and drink

There's a friendly welcome, a riverside garden and good food at The Bucks Head in Meonstoke (open all day at weekends).

What to see

Corhampton church is remarkable in having no dedication, and has remained almost unaltered since it was built in the 11th century. Many Saxon details include 'long and short' stonework at the corners. Note the sundial on the south wall (divided into eight sections not twelve), the 12th-century wall-paintings in the chancel, a 1,000-year-old yew tree and the Romano-British coffin in the churchyard.

BUTSER ANCIENT FARM, CHALTON AND BURITON

DISTANCE/TIME	7.8 miles (12.5km) / 3hrs 45min
ASCENT/GRADIENT	1224ft (373m) / ▲ ▲ ▲
PATHS	Woodland paths, bridleways and forest tracks, 1 stile
LANDSCAPE	Downland forest and farmland
SUGGESTED MAP	AA Walker's Map 20 Chichester & The South Downs
START/FINISH	Grid reference: SU718185
DOG FRIENDLINESS	Dogs can run free in Queen Elizabeth Country Park
PARKING	Pay-and-display car parks at country park
PUBLIC TOILETS	In visitor centre

Queen Elizabeth Country Park lies at the western end of the South Downs and forms part of the East Hampshire Area of Outstanding Natural Beauty. Covering some 1,400 acres (567ha), it is dominated by three hills – the chalk downland of Butser Hill, which at 890ft (271m) is Hampshire's second highest point, and the woodland of Holt Down and War Down. Planted with beech and conifer trees in the 1930s, the woodland is commercially managed and provides excellent recreational facilities.

Along with its informative visitor centre and café, it also provides a useful starting point for longer circular walks and more adventurous hikes along the South Downs Way, the Hangers Way or the Staunton Way. Although this walk makes good use of the country park trails, the emphasis is on exploring the ancient archaeological farm south of the park and two of Hampshire's oldest and most scenic villages, Chalton and Buriton.

Allow time to visit Butser Ancient Farm (closed Sat–Sun, Oct–Mar) near Chalton. Neither a museum nor a theme park, it is an open-air laboratory for archaeology, focusing on the Iron Age (1000 BC–AD 43) and the Roman period (AD 43–400). Through evidence collected from excavations of prehistoric and Roman sites, it has been possible to recreate a full-scale Iron Age settlement using only the materials and tools that ancient people would have had at their disposal. You can wander around earthworks, view inside a Roman villa with a working hypocaust, see the thatched roundhouses and watch demonstrations of iron smelting, pottery making and weaving. Fields are also being cultivated with ancient crops using replica tools, and animals can be seen in the livestock enclosures. You'll find the settlement particularly atmospheric on a quiet day.

Along the lane in Chalton is the thatched Red Lion, reputedly the oldest pub in Hampshire. Visit St Michael's church opposite to see a fine 15th-century font and, from the top corner of the churchyard, a memorable downland view. Explore Buriton before you climb back to the country park. There's a green with a duck pond, attractive cottages, a large church, rectory and manor house.

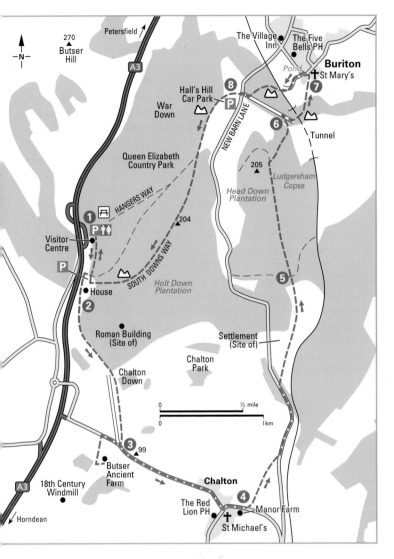

1. From the fingerpost at the car park, follow the 'Short Woodland Trail' (green-booted posts) to the right. On reaching the road, turn right then left and join the gravelled track at a blue-topped horseshoe post. Follow the bridleway ahead past the maintenance yard and a boarded-up house and bear away from the A3 on an overgrown grassy lane.

2. Gently climb between fields on a fenced path, the bridleway soon curving left around woodland, then gradually bear right between fields, noting the 18th-century windmill on the skyline to your right.

3. At the road, turn right to visit Butser Ancient Farm, otherwise turn left and follow the road (some blind bends) for 0.5 miles (800m) into Chalton. Turn left at the junction, signed 'Ditcham'. (Bear right for The Red Lion.)

4. Continue uphill past Manor Farm and, at a fork, bear left along a byway. Continue between fields and soon descend through trees to join a road. Turn left, walking parallel to the railway for 0.25 miles (400m) and past a metal gate, to a stile on the right. Bear slightly left across a large field, pass under electricity lines and enter woodland near the corner of the field

5. At a junction of paths continue straight ahead and steadily climb on a wide forest track. As the track starts to bend left take the grassy fork on the right and start to descend on a sunken footpath and continue down to a road.

6. Turn right on the road and in 22yds (20m), take the footpath left, keep right and head steeply down through the trees to a kissing gate. Bear slightly right across a field on a fenced path to another kissing gate, then follow the path round to the left, between the pond and the church, into Buriton.

7. Turn left along the High Street then left again down South Lane, signed Hangers Way, passing the cemetery on the right and a pretty thatched cottage on the left. The tarmac road becomes a gravel path and starts to climb, pass under a railway bridge and continue up steep path besides the chalk pits. At the road turn right and cross into Hall's Hill car park.

8. Go past a gate and up a wide track (South Downs Way, SDW) back into Queen Elizabeth Country Park. Gradually ascend then, just after a track merges from the right, continue ahead on SDW. Shortly after the path forks again, keep ahead on left fork. At next fingerpost bear right on narrower track (signed SDW). Walk through beech woodland and at a cross tracks continue straight on (signed SDW) as you start to descend. On reaching a T-junction turn right and then at driveway turn left to the visitor centre and car park.

Where to eat and drink

Besides the café in the country park, The Red Lion at Chalton offers Fuller's ales and good views from the rear garden, and The Five Bells in Buriton, which offers an extensive menu. The Village Inn offers breakfast, lunch and dinner and serves aged steaks as well as pub classics.

What to see

Make a point of visiting the Norman church of St Mary in Buriton. The 18th-century historian, Edward Gibbon, best known for his book *The Decline and Fall of the Roman Empire*, lived in the adjacent manor house and is buried in the churchyard. You will also find a memorial window to John Goodyer (1592–1664), one of the first great botanists, who wrote about potatoes and tobacco after they were brought to this country.

While you're there

Visit Petersfield, a market town 3 miles (4.8km) to the north. Its wide main square hosts weekly markets on Wednesday and Saturday, and a monthly farmers market. The little Flora Twort Gallery, just off the main square, is particularly worth seeking out. Twort (1893–1985) was a celebrated watercolour artist, and many of her works depict lively local scenes and people in and around the town. The gallery also showcases items from a rich collection of historic costume started by nearby Bedales School.

HAMBLEDON —
THE CRADLE OF CRICKET

DISTANCE/TIME	6.4 miles (10.25km) / 3hrs
ASCENT/GRADIENT	548ft (167m) / ▲
PATHS	Field paths, farm tracks and stretches of road, 6 stiles
LANDSCAPE	Rolling farmland and chalk downland
SUGGESTED MAP	AA Walker's Map 20 Chichester & The South Downs
START/FINISH	Grid reference: SU646150
DOG FRIENDLINESS	Keep dogs under control at all times
PARKING	Street parking near Hambledon village centre
PUBLIC TOILETS	None on route

Hambledon is steeped in cricketing history. Broadhalfpenny Down, 2 miles (3.2km) north-east of the village, has echoed with the sound of leather on willow since 1750, a time when the game was played with a curved bat and two forked sticks as stumps. Although cricket had been played in other parts of England, it was Hambledon Cricket Club that formulated the rules of the modern game and promoted the growth of club cricket.

Successful club

Hambledon became known as 'the cradle of cricket' through the successes of the club between 1772 and 1781. They won 23 of 39 matches played against All England teams, and became famous throughout the world. Their greatest victory was in 1777 when they won by an innings and 168 runs in a match played for 1,000 guineas. Matches became memorable affairs, with thousands of spectators travelling miles to witness sporting history.

The Bat and Ball pub, built in 1730, served as a pavilion and clubhouse. Landlord Richard Nyren, a great all-rounder, became club captain, secretary, groundsman and an authority on the rules of the game. When Nyren moved to the George Hotel in the village, the club left Broadhalfpenny Down and continued with equal success on Windmill Down.

The gradual decline of Hambledon Cricket Club coincided with the formation of Marylebone Cricket Club in 1787 and the administration of the game moving to Lord's, the London cricket ground established by Thomas Lord, who was president of the Hambledon club at the time. When Nyren left Hambledon in 1791 the club broke up and declined until about 1857, when a ground was established at Ridge Meadow near Park Farm.

Walk here on a summer weekend and you are bound to find a match in progress, either at Ridge Meadow or Broadhalfpenny Down. Relax with a drink outside The Bat and Ball and view the classic English scene. Across the road from the inn you'll find the memorial stone, inscribed with two bats, a ball and stumps, commemorating the prowess of Hambledon Cricket Club, 1750–87.

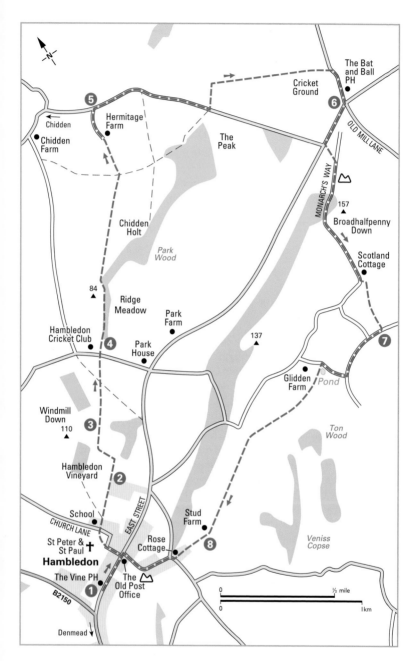

1. From the village hall turn left along the street into the village centre and turn left opposite The Old Post Office towards the parish church. Follow the public footpath to the right, through the churchyard to Church Lane. Take the road opposite, to the right of the primary school, then, where it turns left, keep ahead along the well waymarked public footpath.

2. Cross a drive and proceed straight on between the fruit bushes of Hambledon Vineyard. Cross a stile ahead of you and turn left onto a track. Keep straight on along the footpath. In 65yds (59m), go through a kissing gate on your right and head towards the right-hand edge of trees opposite.

3. Pass through a kissing gate and bear right through the trees into a field. Turn left along the field edge and continue across the field, heading towards two aerials on the horizon, to cross a road via a gap in the hedge. You are now in Ridge Meadow, the modern home of Hambledon Cricket Club

4. Keep to the right-hand edge of the ground and exit in the corner. Walk along a fence dividing two fields. Cross a field, and continue with woodland on your right. At the end of the woods turn right through the hedge, by a waymarker. Go across a large field in a north easterly direction to a gap by a gate. Join a track ahead leading to Hermitage Farm and follow the drive to the road.

5. Turn right and walk for 0.5 miles (800m) to where a footpath crosses the road. Turn left and go left around the field edge then turn at waymarker to walk between two fields. Turn sharp right along the edge of the next field and when the field ends take a few steps to the left and follow adjoining field edge on your right to a stile and the road. Turn right to The Bat and Ball, cricket ground (with its memorial stone) and crossroads.

6. Turn right, then after 250yds (229m), opposite the road to Chidden, cross the stile left. Head uphill across the field to a stile and turn right along a track, waymarked 'Monarch's Way'. Follow the track through a small pine plantation and across Broadhalfpenny Down to Scotland Cottage. Where the drive bears right at the end of the lawn, turn left at the fingerpost and immediately right along a tree-lined path. Descend to a track and turn sharp right at a fingerpost.

7. Go right, then left and after 250yds (229m) turn right along the track to Glidden Farm. Turn left just beyond a pond, cross a stile and go through a gate to bear right at a barn, and keep to the track across fields and two kissing gates. Walk beside telephone poles, through a kissing gate and across a stile and track. Keep alongside the poles to a gate and leave the field. Walk alongside a field and keep left of some fir trees on a grassy track.

8. Go through the gate to the rear of outbuildings (Stud Farm) onto the access road. With your back to the farm, bear right down a narrow path along a paddock to a road next to Rose Cottage. Turn right and keep left steeply downhill back into Hambledon. Turn left through the village back to the village hall.

Where to eat and drink
The Bat and Ball on Broadhalfpenny Down is open all day. In Hambledon, try The Vine Inn (by the village hall).

What to see
The vines at Hambledon benefit from the southeast-facing, chalky slopes, and were first planted in 1952, making this England's oldest commercial vineyard. This successful vineyard helped to change opinions about English wine. In 2005 new Chardonnay, Pinot Noir and Pinot Meunier stock was planted, marking a shift towards the production of sparkling wines.

WICKHAM AND THE FOREST OF BERE

DISTANCE/TIME	4 miles (6.4km) / 2hrs
ASCENT/GRADIENT	226ft (69m) / ▲
PATHS	Bridleways and forest tracks – will be muddy after rain
LANDSCAPE	Old railway path, river valley and mature woodland
SUGGESTED MAP	OS Explorer OL3 Meon Valley, Portsmouth, Gosport & Fareham
START/FINISH	Grid reference: SU574116
DOG FRIENDLINESS	Run free on the old railway and in West Walk
PARKING	Station car park, Wickham
PUBLIC TOILETS	Station Road, Wickham

With its medieval market square and engaging collection of independent shops, Wickham is one of Hampshire's most attractive little towns. It was the birthplace of William of Wykeham, founder of both Winchester College and New College, Oxford.

Despite his humble peasant background, William led a charmed life, and by the time he was appointed Bishop of Winchester in 1367 he was a wealthy man. He transformed the interior of his great Norman cathedral and personally endowed the two prestigious colleges that still flourish more than 600 years after his death. William had been educated in Winchester, where he caught the eye of Bishop Edington, who introduced him to Edward III.

In a secular career spanning 20 years, William rose to be Chief Surveyor of the Royal Castles and Warden of Forests and Woods. It was a fitting appointment, for in those days Wickham lay at the heart of the Forest of Bere, a vast woodland stretching from the Sussex border to the River Test. Saxon kings hunted here long before the Norman Conquest, but in 1086 King William formally declared Bere to be a royal hunting forest. However, when Charles I led the last royal hunt in 1628, most of the trees had been felled to provide timber for the naval dockyards along the south coast.

Timber remains an important industry and a large timber yard still flourishes beside the former railway goods yard at Mislingford. The Meon Valley railway arrived late on the Hampshire landscape, a product of territorial skirmishing between the London & South Western Railway and its arch-rival, the Great Western. In an effort to protect its south-coast traffic from the Great Western railheads at Basingstoke and Winchester, the LSWR opened its own route from Alton to Fareham in 1903.

Built to mainline standards with gentle curves and easy gradients, the new line was an expensive white elephant. From the start it generated little revenue, drifting through the interwar years towards its inevitable closure in 1955. Yet the Meon Valley railway has its place in history. Early in June 1944,

Sir Winston Churchill and his war cabinet met other Allied leaders in a special train at Droxford Station to complete their plans for the D-Day invasion of Europe. With working trains now a distant memory, much of the old line has a new role as a peaceful bridleway. This walk follows the old line up the valley before plunging into West Walk, a charming mixture of 19th-century oak and modern conifer plantations that forms the largest surviving fragment of the former Royal forest. The area is now a forest nature reserve, with a variety of visitor facilities.

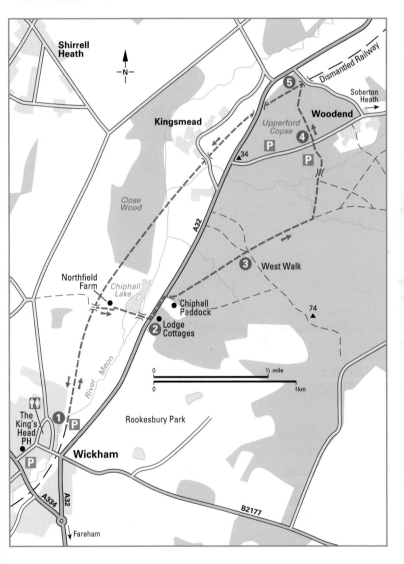

1. The station car park on the northeast outskirts of Wickham backs directly onto the bridleway. Turn left, heading north and leaving the bridge over the River Meon behind you. Follow the old line as far as the first overbridge; 60yds (55m) beyond the brick arch, take the path that doubles back to the left and climb up to the farm track at the top. Turn left, cross over the bridge and follow the track as it winds past Northfield Farm and Chiphall Lake trout fishery to the A32.

2. There is no footway here so cross carefully over, turn left, and take great care as you follow the busy main road for 200yds (183m), passing two lodge cottages on the right-hand side. 150yds (137m) further on, turn right past a wooden barrier into West Walk. Follow the grassy track at right angles to the road for the first 75yds (69m), then fork left onto a forest path, stepping over a large fallen tree. Ignore all turnings and keep ahead as the trail dips into a small valley, crosses a brook, and climbs to a five-way junction.

3. Keep ahead here, downhill, signed towards West Walk and Woodend. Continue along the gravelled path and at the next crossways (signed 'Woodend') fork left onto a slightly narrower gravel track. Follow this ahead, dropping down to cross a footbridge. Climb the hill up through Woodend car park, crossing the Soberton Heath road via a small gate. Go through a barrier opposite into Upperford Copse.

4. Walk straight downhill through the woods, following the 'Soberton and Newtown Millennium Walk' sign. At cross tracks at the bottom of the hill continue ahead to reach the former railway line at a bridge.

5. Join the old line immediately south of the road bridge and head left, passing under another bridge carrying the A32, for 2 miles (3.2km), back to the start.

Where to eat and drink

Wickham has a good choice of pubs, restaurants and tearooms, including The King's Head for Fuller's ales and home-cooked specials, and the recently renovated 15th-century Square Cow. Light lunches and afternoon teas are served at Lilly's Tea and Coffee House.

What to see

The lavish scale of the bridges and earthworks along the old railway path tell their own tale of thwarted ambition. Although the line was built wide enough for double track, it opened with just a single line – and traffic was so disappointing that the second track was never laid.

While you're there

Children will love exploring the secret tunnels and underground chambers at the fully restored Fort Nelson. One of a chain of Victorian forts on Portsdown Hill, it was built to defend Portsmouth from the threat of a Napoleonic invasion that never came. The fort is open daily throughout the year (except Christmas) with guided tours and family events. Refreshments are available in Café 1871.

BREAMORE AND THE MIZ MAZE

DISTANCE/TIME	5.5 miles (8.9km) / 2hrs 30min
ASCENT/GRADIENT	387ft (118m) / ▲
PATHS	Field paths, minor roads, woodland trails, 2 stiles
LANDSCAPE	Woodland and farmland on the New Forest fringe
SUGGESTED MAP	OS Explorer OL22 New Forest
START/FINISH	Grid reference: SU157178
DOG FRIENDLINESS	Under control at all times
PARKING	Car park at primary school, Breamore
PUBLIC TOILETS	Opposite Countryside Museum (when the house is open)

Breamore, pronounced 'Bremmer', is a truly ancient settlement. Stretching across the lush water-meadows and up the western chalk slopes of the Avon Valley, it is also one of Hampshire's most impressive villages with lots to recommend it in terms of both beauty and history. First-time visitors will be enthralled by the knots of 17th-century brick-built cottages and farmhouses, mostly thatched and timber-framed, which are dotted around a large boggy common and, close to Breamore's centrepiece, the fine Elizabethan manor house.

Saxon survivor

The main village attractions are the manor, the Saxon church and the Countryside Museum. This walk climbs Breamore Down to the mystical Miz Maze and a prehistoric long barrow.

The church of St Mary, close to Breamore House, is a rare Saxon survivor, having been built about AD 980. Despite later alterations, including a Norman porch and a 14th-century chancel, it still preserves much of the Saxon fabric, notably the extensive use of flints and some Roman bricks in its construction, small double-splayed windows, an Anglo-Saxon inscription and a magnificent Saxon stone rood above the nave doorway. There's much of interest here, so pick up a copy of the guide book before you explore.

The pre-Reformation church was closely linked with Breamore Priory (1130–1536). The site can be seen beside the Avon just north of Breamore Mill. Following the dissolution of the priory, a manor was built in 1583 by Queen Elizabeth's treasurer, William Doddington. In warm red brick in the classic Elizabethan 'E' shape, it was purchased in the 18th century by Sir Edward Hulse, King George II's physician, and has remained the Hulse family home ever since.

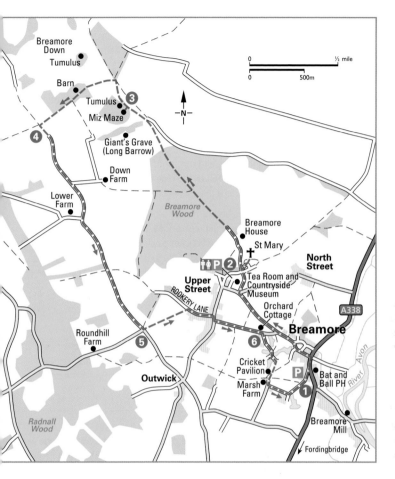

1. Turn right out of the car park exit and walk along the main road to the lane on your left, signed to Breamore House, opposite Hulse Hall. When the road bears left go right, signed for Breamore House, and continue up the lane to a T-junction. Take the driveway opposite and then bear right at the gate to Breamore House, to visit the church of St Mary.

2. After visiting the church, walk back through the churchyard and take the bridleway on your right, walking back to the gates of Breamore House (push button entry) and up the drive towards the house. Pass the house and keep ahead, leaving the stables on your right as you ascend the track into Breamore Wood. Keep to the main path as it curves right, then left (by a fingerpost) soon after leaving the trees at the crest of the hill. Bear left at a fork on the edge of rough grassland and keep ahead along a permissive path as far as a sign to the Miz Maze.

3. Turn left into the dense hilltop yew grove to discover the turf-cut Miz Maze. Returning to Point 3, leave the copse, turn left along the grassy swathe back down to the bridleway, and turn left. After 100yds (91m), turn left through a waymarked kissing gate and walk down the left-hand field edge. Keep ahead

as the path joins a track through woodland and continue past a metal barn. As the main track bears left (private), continue ahead on grassy track, walking along the woodland edge and down the side of the next field to a stile.

4. Cross the stile and turn left onto the bridleway, which soon merges with a gravelled track. Pass a metal barrier and keep ahead past the turning to Down Farm on your left. Continue walking past Lower Farm on your right, until you reach a metalled lane.

5. Turn left and when the path divides turn right into a field, heading diagonally across a field. Crest the brow of the hill and continue towards a thatched cottage, then pass through a gate and turn right onto a metalled lane. Turn right then left at the bottom and follow the lane to a gravel path on the right, opposite Orchard Cottage.

6. Follow this path as it twists and turns to a small clearing with two houses. Turn left through a gate and over a plank bridge, then turn right across the field, passing in front of the thatched cricket pavilion on your right. Join the gravel track in front of Marsh Farm and at the junction bear left. Follow the track, passing behind the primary school, and back to find the car park exit on your right.

Where to eat and drink

Light lunches and afternoon tea are served at the tearoom in the courtyard outside the Countryside Museum from noon (Easter–October (when the house is open). Call in at the Bat and Ball in Breamore or the Horse and Groom at nearby Woodgreen.

What to see

The Miz Maze is a quartered labyrinth similar in design to the labyrinth at Chartres Cathedral. Legends about its origins abound, one associating it with monks from Breamore Priory, who had to crawl around the maze on their hands and knees as a penance. Surrounded by a yew copse, the circular maze is about 85ft (26m) in diameter, and is a sacred site for pagans.

While you're there

Completed in 1583, Breamore House is a fine example of an Elizabethan manor house. It has been in the same family for nine generations, and their collected possessions now form the contents of the mansion. The house has been used as a period location in several films. Open selected days, April–October.

AROUND ROMAN ROCKBOURNE

DISTANCE/TIME	5 miles (8.1km) / 2hrs 15min
ASCENT/GRADIENT	515ft (157m) / ▲
PATHS	Field paths, woodland bridleways and tracks, 9 stiles
LANDSCAPE	Rolling fields, areas of woodland
SUGGESTED MAP	OS Explorer OL22 New Forest
START/FINISH	Grid reference: SU113184
DOG FRIENDLINESS	Off lead in woodland, but keep under close control on farmland
PARKING	Rockbourne village hall car park can be used but with prior consent only (bookings@rockbournevillagehall.org.uk)
PUBLIC TOILETS	None on route

The long, gently winding main street in Rockbourne is said to be one of the prettiest in Hampshire. This peaceful and sheltered village is tucked in rolling downland on the borders with Wiltshire and Dorset, and the road is lined with Tudor and Georgian houses and thatched and timber-framed cottages.

The oldest known homestead is the Roman villa, discovered south of the village by a farmer in 1942. He unearthed oyster shells and tiles and the significance of the find was recognised by local antiquarian A T Morley Hewitt, whose first excavation hole revealed a mosaic floor. In 1956, after Morley Hewitt had bought the land, a full-scale excavation began, and the site is one of the most interesting Roman villa complexes to be discovered in the country.

Roman legacy

The Romans established prosperous farm estates with a villa at the centre, most notably in southern England where the soils were fertile. Excavations at Rockbourne identified over 70 rooms, including a pre-Roman circular hut and elaborate bathhouses with underfloor heating. A treasure trove of Roman remains was also uncovered – mosaics, coins, ironwork, jewellery and shards of pottery. Morley Hewitt's detailed study of the site has revealed much about the everyday life of the Roman Britons at Rockbourne. The excavations have been filled in for their own protection, but you can see the outlines of the rooms and buildings marked out in the grass, the hypocaust heating systems and some mosaics.

The walk takes in the neighbouring village of Whitsbury, where foundations of a Roman building, containing a hypocaust and New Forest pottery of the 2nd and 3rd century AD, were found in a field between the church and Glebe House. There is also evidence of even earlier habitation in the village. At the northern end of the village, by Whitsbury Stud, is a fine example of a fortified Iron Age camp.

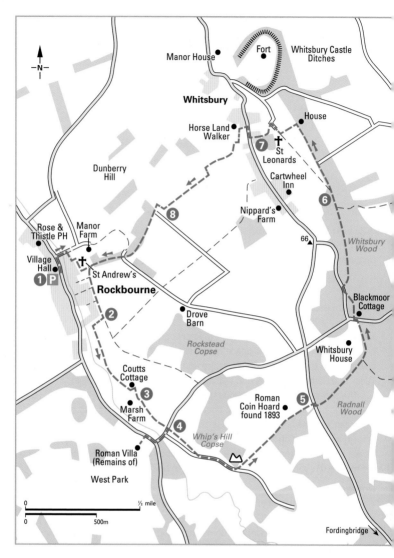

1. Turn left out of the village hall car park and soon take the lane right towards Manor Farm. Turn right, signed to the church, and cross the gravel drive, in front of a white house, to turn right up a stepped path to St Andrew's church. Continue along below the churchyard to reach a junction of paths. Keep straight on behind the school and houses, ignoring three paths on the right, then cross a stile and turn immediately right to go through a gate.

2. Follow the field edge down to the bottom corner and a junction of paths. Turn left and cross a stile to a gate near an electricity substation and take the narrow path ahead over a barrier. Walk through a paddock to the next stile and through the next paddock to a lane. Continue ahead, along the edge of a meadow, to a stile. Pass over the stile and out of the gate in front of Coutts Cottage to reach a track, opposite Marsh Farm.

3. Head left and then immediately right through a gate and continue along the right-hand field edge, next to the farmhouse, to a gate. Continue to another gate, then straight on between fenced fields, passing through a gate to reach a stile and lane. To visit the Roman villa, turn right to a T-junction, and turn right, then left, to the entrance. Afterwards, retrace your steps to rejoin the walk.

4. Take the track opposite, and walk ahead along a wooded track then, at a junction of tracks, take the arrowed path left up a steep bank and over a stile into a field. Follow the path parallel to the field edge to reach a stile at the corner of a wood. Cross a track, and continue downhill inside the woodland edge to a lane.

5. Turn right, then left, along a bridleway, opposite a driveway, and gently climb through Radnall Wood. At a junction bear left (following the blue arrow) and pass behind Whitsbury House to a lane. Turn left, then right, along a track between properties to a lane. Turn right, then bear right along the bridleway through Whitsbury Wood.

6. At a junction with a track, bear left and walk beside several fenced paddocks to a house and large barn. Turn left along a track between the paddocks towards St Leonard's church. Turn left at the T-junction and soon after enter the churchyard. Go through the gate opposite the church door and descend to the lane.

7. Turn left for the Cartwheel Inn, otherwise turn right, then left, along a farm drive and keep ahead, bearing left at the horse land walker, then right between paddocks, uphill to a kissing gate. Turn left along the field edge, and then soon after turn right and head across the field to a track.

8. Turn right and follow the track as it bears left to a junction of tracks. Go through the gate opposite and then walk back to St Andrew's church. Retrace your steps back to the village hall.

Where to eat and drink
The Rose and Thistle in Rockbourne is a thatched 16th-century building with an unspoilt interior. In Whitsbury, the Cartwheel Inn is noted for its real ales, home-cooked food and peaceful garden.

What to see
Interesting memorials to the Coote family, who lived at West Park to the south of the village, can be seen in St Andrew's church in Rockbourne. Lieutenant-General Sir Eyre Coote was the most famous, distinguishing himself as one of Clive of India's officers at the Battle of Plassey, in Bengal, in 1757. He is buried in the church and a 100ft (30m) monument was erected in West Park by the East India Company in 1828 to commemorate him, seen shortly after Point 4, to the southwest.

While you're there
Visit the museum at the Roman Villa (open Easter to September), which displays many of the artefacts, explains its development, and describes what life would have been like on this large Roman farm. (Dogs allowed on site.)

A NEW FOREST
WALK FROM FRITHAM

DISTANCE/TIME	5.7 miles (9.2km) / 2hrs 30min
ASCENT/GRADIENT	361ft (110m) / ▲
PATHS	Gravel forest tracks, heathland and woodland paths
LANDSCAPE	Ancient woodland and open heathland
SUGGESTED MAP	AA Walker's Map 3 New Forest
START/FINISH	Grid reference: SU230141
DOG FRIENDLINESS	Great for dogs, but keep under strict control around wildlife and cyclists
PARKING	Forestry Commission car park beyond Royal Oak
PUBLIC TOILETS	None on route

Fritham is an unspoilt commoning community nestling in a remote and peaceful enclave of pasture within the boundaries of the New Forest National Park. A scattering of cottages and farms, a chapel and a charming thatched pub are all that line the winding dead-end lane that leads straight on to the gorse- and heather-covered Fritham Plain. Many of the old cottages in the village have Forest Rights, which entitle the owners or tenants to graze cattle, horses and donkeys on the open forest, and to collect turf and wood for fuel. Pannage or Mast Rights also allow pigs to forage for acorns and beech masts in autumn to prevent the ponies from eating too many. These rights and the traditional commoners' way of life have existed for over 900 years. Here, on the forest fringe, you are likely to see domestic livestock, including enormous pigs, wandering, foraging and mixing with the New Forest ponies.

A shattered peace

Fritham has not always been an idyllic rural scene. Its peace was shattered in 1865 when a German, Eduard Schultze, opened a gunpowder factory in an isolated glade beside the tree-fringed Eyeworth Pond or Irons Well. Fritham's remote setting and the ready availability of charcoal, the main constituent of black gunpowder, made it an ideal location. Tracks from the village were strengthened to take the huge carts and the river was dammed to provide water power for the mills. As demand for smokeless sporting gunpowder increased, so the factory grew, eventually employing over 100 people from as far afield as Fordingbridge. After supplying gunpowder during World War I, the factory was sold in 1923 and the operation was moved to Scotland. Things went quiet for time – but, early in World War II, 4,000 acres (1,620ha) of nearby heathland were enclosed to create the Ashley Walk bombing range. Within its 9-mile (14.5km) perimeter fence, the site was a maze of natural and artificial targets that included bunkers, trenches and steel plates, as well as two massive concrete walls at Cockley Plain and Leaden Hall. The range was the testing ground for a wide variety of military hardware, including the largest bomb to be dropped in England and the famous 'Dam Buster' bouncing bomb. Over 400 craters were counted on aerial photos taken after the range closed in 1946. Now, more than 60 years later, the small brick observation shelter that you'll see near Ashley Cross is the only remaining building left standing from this time.

1. Turn left out of the car park and head downhill along the road.

2. Keep ahead at the foot of the hill, crossing the bridge at Eyeworth Pond, and follow the short gravel track to a low wooden barrier at Oak Tree Cottage. Leave the barrier on your left, take the narrow but well defined path that heads north into Eyeworth Wood, and follow it for 0.5 miles (800m).

3. After a while, the path leads onto a tree-studded heath, with far-reaching views. Continue for a further 550yds (503m) across Homy Ridge, on the main track, as far as a stocky Scots pine tree standing at the edge of a small wood on your right.

4. The path divides here. Take the left-hand fork, and walk down into an open grassy valley and then up the other side to the car park at Telegraph Hill.

5. Turn left beside the B3078 for 20yds (18m), before turning left again onto the gravel track directly opposite Hope Cottage. The track bears left soon after passing a small, seasonal pond at Studley Head and dives briefly beneath holly and oak trees before breaking back out onto the heath.

6. Continue past a small pond on your right, just a few paces beyond the low mound of a tumulus. Follow the track south towards Amberwood Inclosure, ignoring tracks to the left and the path that branches off to your right near Ashley Bottom. A little further on, look for the World War II brick observation shelter, located on your right.

7. As you reach the trees, turn left at a waymarked junction with the cycle track on the edge of Amberwood Inclosure, and dive steeply down the well-made gravel track into the woods. Ignore all turnings and follow the waymarked route through the forest and over the bridge at Latchmoor Brook. Continue on the main track, bearing left just after the bridge. The trees gradually drop behind as the cycle track winds its way up through the trees, and there are glimpses of Eyeworth Lodge away to your left. A steady climb brings you to the green at Fritham. Turn right to return to the car park.

Where to eat and drink
With its thatch, scrubbed pine tables and relaxed, informal garden, The Royal Oak is the perfect retreat before or after your walk. Ringwood tops the list of local ales, and the down-to-earth menu includes home-made pies, local sausages and winter soups, as well as ploughman's lunches. The pub is open all day at weekends and during school holidays.

What to see
Note the metal postbox by the car park entrance. Placed here before 1900, it saved the postman his journey to the gunpowder factory and surrounding cottages. Look out too for deer. The New Forest owes its existence to deer as it was originally established by William the Conqueror in 1079 as a royal hunting ground. The fallow deer you are likely to see on the walk are directly descended from the beasts of the chase 900 years ago. The heather and gorse are also home to one of Britain's rarest heathland birds, the Dartford warbler.

While you're there
Visit the Rufus Stone, between Brook and the A31. Erected in 1841, it is said to mark the spot where William Rufus (William II, the Conquerer's son), was killed accidentally while out hunting in 1100.

CHURCH TREASURES AT MINSTEAD

DISTANCE/TIME	5.3 miles (8.6km) / 2hrs 30min
ASCENT/GRADIENT	554ft (169m) / ▲
PATHS	Field paths, bridleways, forest tracks, roads, 5 stiles
LANDSCAPE	Pasture and farmland, forest inclosures and heathland
SUGGESTED MAP	AA Walker's Map 3 New Forest
START/FINISH	Grid reference: SU280109
DOG FRIENDLINESS	Let them off lead on heathland
PARKING	Minstead church or by village green
PUBLIC TOILETS	None on route

Of the New Forest's half-dozen delightful villages, enchanting Minstead is among the most visited and the least spoiled. Completely encircled by forest, with thatched and weatherboarded cottages nestling in a maze of high-banked lanes, it is one of those communities which seem completely isolated from the outside world, the lush landscape of rolling pasture and scattered woodland contrasting with the ancient surrounding forest.

Whitby in miniature

Referred to as Mintestede – 'the place where mint grows' – in the *Domesday Book*, the village has remained relatively untroubled since William Rufus was killed while out hunting at nearby Canterton Glen in 1100. Crowning a little hill overlooking the village is the church of All Saints, one of the hidden treasures of the county, which dates back to at least the 13th century. Originally thatched and looking more like a cottage, with its series of different-sized gables, dormers and attractive little extensions, it has immediate appeal and you should allow time to explore its fascinating interior and churchyard. According to Pevsner, its wealth of old furniture and fittings is surpassed only by St Mary's at Whitby, North Yorkshire.

All Saints is built of traditional New Forest materials, wattle filled in with rubble and daub, with stone only spared for the arches and quoins in the main walls. Beyond the porch and the arched main doorway, ancient wooden door and deeply worn step that has seen the passing of worshippers and pilgrims for over 800 years, you will find a surprisingly intact Georgian interior. Note the rare and unusual three-decker pulpit, made of oak and patched with pine, dating from the 17th century. The lowest deck was used by the parish clerk who said the 'Amens'; the middle deck was where the scriptures were read and the sermon was preached from the upper level. The fine nave is filled with a double tier of galleries, built in the 18th century to accommodate musicians and the growing congregation, with the plain upper gallery added to provide free seating for children and the poor of the parish. You will also find the

17th-century box pews of interest, in particular the three family pews for the local gentry, each with their own entrance and one equipped like a cosy sitting room with comfortable seating and a fireplace. If you take a stroll around the churchyard you'll find the grave of the best-known Minstead resident, Sir Arthur Conan Doyle (1869–1930), and his wife on the south side by an oak tree. He created Sherlock Holmes and lived at nearby Bignell Wood.

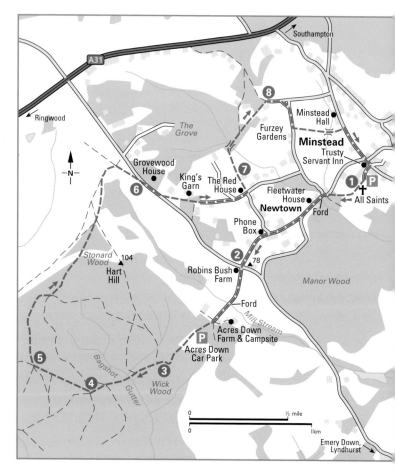

1. Go through a kissing gate to the right of the churchyard and walk down to another gate. Continue on a fenced path to enter a wood. Exit the wood via a gate, bear right and then left on to the road. Cross the ford and keep to the lane, bearing left by a disused phone box, now a community library.

2. At a crossroads, go straight over, following the sign to 'Acres Down'. Cross a ford, then, at the crossroads just past the farm, bear right. Almost immediately take the left fork along a track, signed 'Acres Down Car Park'. Walk past the car park and a low gate on the broad gravel track.

3. Stay on the track as it first bends left and then swings sharp right between gateposts. Ignore the track on the right, keep ahead and descend to cross a

small stream, and continue for 380yds (347m) to a crossways at the top of a gentle slope.

4. Turn right, by markerpost 99, then immediately left into a young conifer and birch woodland. Crest a rise, going down beside mature conifers on the right.

5. At a junction of five tracks turn right, still on a wide gravel track. As the track bends right and before it starts to rise, turn left on a sandy track that gently rises, passing an open area to the right and wire fence to the left. Pass through a gap in the fence to emerge at a grassy five-track meeting point. Take the second right through the wood and emerge on the edge of heathland. Turn right and soon merge with gravel track coming from the right. Follow this through a small patch of woodland onto the edge of the heath. Swing right, to reach the road.

6. Cross over and walk left down the verge. Pass Grovewood House and turn left down the bridleway, signed to King's Garn. Pass the house, take the left fork and join the track merging from the right, keeping to the left. Continue downhill and just before reaching a road, turn left over a stile and continue between boundaries.

7. Drop down and up to a stile. Enter woodland and immediately turn right down the slope at a waymarker post. Cross a stream on a footbridge and go along a stepped boardwalk then fork right through a kissing gate. Cross a plank bridge, go through a kissing gate and continue a gentle ascent. Join a path from the right and go ahead into a car park. Fork right past Furzey Gardens and down to the road.

8. Turn right, then right again and again. Take the footpath left over the stile and walk along the left-hand field-edge to a bridge and stile. Maintain direction through the next field to a stile by a gate onto a road. Turn right into Minstead, then right after the pub, back to the church.

Where to eat and drink
The Trusty Servant Inn in Minstead has an extensive menu, good real ale and accommodation. Refreshments are also available in the Gallery Gift and Coffee Shop at Furzey Gardens, which is free to enter.

What to see
Note the unusual pub sign which depicts the 'trusty servant', a swine-snouted character with a padlocked jaw to illustrate his discretion and stag's feet to indicate his speed in running errands. The original 16th-century picture and inscription (in Latin) hangs in Winchester College.

While you're there
Visit Furzey Gardens (no dogs), 8 acres (3.2ha) of glades around a thatched cottage dating from 1560. You can see winter and summer heathers, rare flowering trees and shrubs, extensive collections of rhododendrons and azaleas, and a wonderful display of spring bulbs.

LYNDHURST'S PARK PALE

DISTANCE/TIME	3.4 miles (5.5km) / 1hr 30min
ASCENT/GRADIENT	164ft (50m) / ▲
PATHS	Heath and forest tracks, muddy woodland bridleway and roadside pavements
LANDSCAPE	New Forest heath and deciduous woodland
SUGGESTED MAP	AA Walker's Map 3 New Forest
START/FINISH	Grid reference: SU303081
DOG FRIENDLINESS	On lead along roads and near grazing animals
PARKING	Bolton's Bench car park
PUBLIC TOILETS	In the main car park, Lyndhurst

Legend has it that Lyndhurst's Park Pale was originally built to round up the deer to make them easier targets for William II, whose aim is reputed to have been less than perfect.

The story has rather shaky foundations, since the Park Pale was first recorded in 1291 and, although this vast earthwork was already old by then, the date is almost two centuries after William's death in 1100. Whether or not King William was the inspiration for the work, its purpose is not in dispute. Building the Park Pale involved digging several miles of ditch and earth bank and this major construction project amply demonstrates the importance of venison in medieval times. After more than 700 years of erosion, about 3.4 miles (5.5km) of earthworks are still marked on modern maps and the original structure may have been significantly longer. Even today, the structure is as much as 29ft (8.8m) wide in places and the bank is up to 4ft (1.2m) high. When topped by the original wooden paling fence, Park Pale would have been a very effective barrier to even the most agile deer.

The existing structure has a wide, open entrance adjoining the present Park Ground Inclosure, with earthworks that curve around to a narrow closed neck not far from the start of your walk. Deer driven in from the entrance would soon have found themselves trapped and presented an easy target to the marksmen at the opposite end. You'll walk beside part of this section not long after setting out and cross it as you drop down to the Beaulieu Road.

Hotel with a history

After crossing the road, you'll follow a bridleway with views to the Lime Wood Hotel. In the 13th century this was the site of a royal hunting lodge that was rebuilt by the Duke of Clarence in 1740. The building was modernised again a century later, when visitors included Queen Victoria and her family. Then, in 1880, Mr Willingham Rawnsley a brother of Canon Rawnsley, one of the founders of the National Trust, established a boys' school here. Later, the house became a hotel but was requisitioned for military use in World War II, when it played a part in the preparations for D-Day.

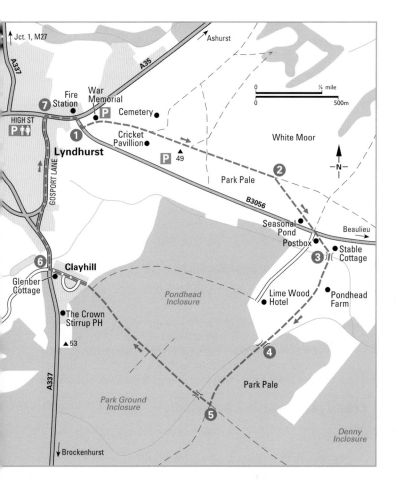

1. Start at the war memorial and follow the tarmac road towards the thatched cricket pavilion, when it bears left to the cemetery keep straight ahead on a gravel track. Continue ahead, as it slowly rises for just over half a mile (800m).

2. As the main track starts to bear left take unmarked but well-defined winding path on the right and descend across the low earthworks of Park Pale towards a red postbox. Cross the road beside a small seasonal pond and take the left-hand fork towards Pondhead Farm.

3. Bear right past the drive to Little Boston and Stable Cottage. Cross the white-railed bridge, then fork right at Pondhead Farm, around the wooden barrier. Keep ahead past the house on your right, following the woodland bridleway, with views towards the Lime Wood Hotel beyond the fence on your right. Keep ahead along a path in the trees alongside the field behind the hotel. Bear left over plank bridge.

4. Cross the footbridge and bear right, keeping within sight of the wire fence on your right, until you meet a gravelled track crossing your path.

5. Turn right, cross the bridge and follow this appealing forest track through stands of beech, oak and silver birch. Continue through a wooden gate but turn

left on the path just after the gate to visit The Crown Stirrup pub, and keep ahead along the residential Beechen Lane to the A337.

6. Turn right along the roadside pavement and fork right along Gosport Lane, where the pavement continues on the other side, as far as the T-junction with Lyndhurst High Street.

7. Turn right and right again opposite the fire station, to return to the car park.

Where to eat and drink

The Crown Stirrup is a country pub on the outskirts of Lyndhurst serving real ales and home-cooked food. There's a garden with a play area, too. Alternatively, you'll find plenty of choice in Lyndhurst itself. Try The Lyndhurst Tea House or Willow Tree Café, both on the High Street. There are also several other High Street pubs and tearooms to choose from.

What to see

More than 4,000 New Forest ponies graze the lawns and trees on the heath and scrub near Allum Green and Poundhill Heath. They are descendants of a wild breed peculiar to the New Forest and belong to local commoners.

While you're there

Visit Alice Liddell's grave in St Michaels and All Angels churchyard. Alice became the inspiration for *Alice in Wonderland* after meeting the Reverend Charles Dodgson (alias author Lewis Carroll) in Oxford, when she was just a little girl. In 1880 Alice married Reginald Hargreaves and moved to Cuffnells, near Lyndhurst. Following her death in 1934, her ashes were interred in the family grave.

DISCOVERING NEW FOREST TRAILS

DISTANCE/TIME	9.5 miles (15.3km) / 4hrs 30 min
ASCENT/GRADIENT	440ft (134m) / ▲
PATHS	Grass and gravel forest tracks, heathland paths, some roads
LANDSCAPE	Ornamental Drive, ancient forest inclosures and heathland
SUGGESTED MAP	AA Walker's Map 3 New Forest
START/FINISH	Grid reference: SU266057
DOG FRIENDLINESS	Keep dogs under control at all times
PARKING	Brock Hill Forestry Commission car park, just off A35
PUBLIC TOILETS	Blackwater car park

A short drive southwest of Lyndhurst are ancient woods of oak and beech, notably Bolderwood, and the 19th-century conifer plantation of the Rhinefield Ornamental Drive. You are in the heart of the New Forest and this loop walk explores these contrasting landscapes. A stroll through the rhododendron-lined Ornamental Drive, with its magnificent tall trees and arboretum, takes you through the forest's finest unenclosed and 'inclosed' deciduous woods.

Finest relics of woodland

Unenclosed woodlands such as Whitley Wood are among the finest relics of unspoilt deciduous forest in Western Europe. Hummocky green lawns and paths meander beneath giant beech trees and beside stands of ancient holly and contorted oaks. Inclosures are managed woodlands where young trees are protected from deer and ponies. Areas of oak trees were first inclosed in the late 17th century to provide timber for the construction and shipbuilding industries. Holidays Hill Inclosure, dating from 1676, contains 300-year-old oak trees that matured after iron replaced wood in the shipbuilding industry. Marvel at the 24ft (7.3m) girth of the most famous and probably the oldest tree in the forest, the Knightwood Oak, near the start of the walk. Believed to be 350 years old, it owes its great age to pollarding (cutting back) its limbs to encourage new branches for fuel and charcoal. Pollarding was made illegal in 1698 as fully grown trees were needed to provide timber for shipbuilding, so any tree that shows signs of having been pollarded is of a great age.

Close to Millyford Bridge and Highland Water is the Portugese Fireplace, a memorial to a Portugese army unit, deployed during World War I to cut timber for pit-props. The flint fireplace was used in their cookhouse. Returning through Holidays Hill Inclosure you will join a 'reptile trail' and several marker posts, each carved with a British reptile, lead you to the Reptile Centre. Set up to breed rarer species for the wild, including the smooth snake and sand lizard, it allows you to view some of the forest's more elusive inhabitants.

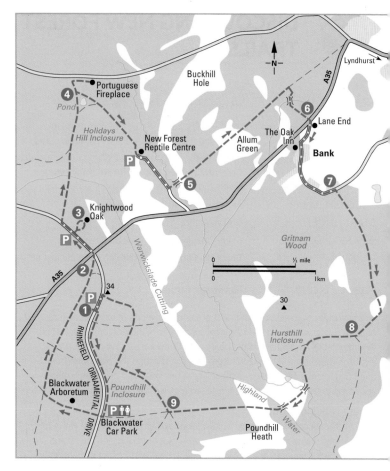

1. Locate the Tall Trees Trail post at the southern end of the car park and follow the path to the road and cross straight over. Keep to the gravel trail (marked by white-banded posts) as it curves right and runs parallel with the road. Pass through an impressive mixed wooded area. The path meanders gently downhill to Blackwater car park, passing several sculptured information panels along the way. At the car park turn right through the rustic arch, cross the road and follow the track towards the arboretum. Go through a gate into the arboretum. Exit by the far gate and keep to the gravel track to a crossing of tracks. Turn right at waymarker post 244 and keep ahead on this track, ignoring paths left and right.

2. As the path bends to the right, take the grassy path on the left, emerging at the junction of roads. Cross over the A35 (take care), go through a gate and follow the road to the car park. Turn right, opposite the car park and follow the well-defined path to the Knightwood Oak.

3. Return towards the car park and bear right along the road. Turn right again after a few paces, onto a path into mixed woodland. Cross a stream and soon reach a gravel track. Bear right, and keep to this track, ignoring all tracks left

and right until reaching a small pond at a triangle of tracks. Bear left onto the gravel cycle route and keep ahead until reaching a gate and road. Turn right to view the Portuguese Fireplace (300yds/274m).

4. Return through the gate to the triangle of tracks. Bear left and follow this to the New Forest Reptile Centre. Walk along the access drive past a cottage dated 1811 then, at a barrier on your left 0.5 miles (800m) further on, drop down onto a path and follow it across a bridge.

5. Keep to the main path for 0.75 miles (1.2km), skirting the walls to Allum Green. Keeping right, cross deeply rutted old forestry tracks in a clearing, and follow a wide grassy path that narrows and gently climbs through trees to a defined crossing of paths and turn right just beyond a large, scorched fallen tree and a ford. Bear slightly right across a clearing and concrete footbridge, then continue through the woodland to a stile beside a gate. Cross the stile to reach the A35.

6. Cross the road and take the lane into Bank to reach The Oak Inn. Continue on the lane through the hamlet.

7. Just beyond the cattle grid, turn right through a gate onto a gravelled cycle track. Follow this track for nearly a mile (1.6km) through a gate to an open area. Continue ahead on main track as it bears right to a junction at a small green.

8. Fork right, and enter Hursthill Inclosure at a gate. Drop down past a turning on the right, then climb again and bear left at a fork. Keep to the waymarked track as it drops past another turning on the right and leaves the inclosure at a gate. Walk over a large wooden bridge next to a 'dead' forest on your left and along the straight track to the bridges over Highland Water, and follow the track around to the right. Soon a gate leads into Poundhill Inclosure, and another straight section brings you to a five-way junction at waymarker post 250.

9. Turn right here. Ignore all turnings and follow the track as it turns sharp right and winds its way to a junction with Rhinefield Ornamental Drive. Turn left for the last 100 yards (91m) back to the car park.

Where to eat and drink

Aim to make it to The Oak Inn at Bank for lunch. A traditional pub, it offers ale from the cask and decent food.

What to see

At the bottom of Rhinefield Ornamental Drive stands the Rhinefield House Hotel, a flamboyant Jacobean-style house, built in 1890 on the site of a hunting lodge used by Charles II. Planted informally in the mid-19th century with exotic trees such as Wellingtonias, redwoods, black spruce and Spanish fir, the Ornamental Drive has reached maturity, and some of the trees are the largest of their species in Britain.

While you're there

Visit the New Forest Centre in Lyndhurst, which brings to life the history, traditions and wildlife of the New Forest. Take a trip up the Bolderwood Ornamental Drive and visit the deer sanctuary near Bolderwood car park.

BURSLEDON AND THE RIVER HAMBLE

34

DISTANCE/TIME	5.9 miles (9.5km) / 2hrs 30min
ASCENT/GRADIENT	331ft (101m) / ▲
PATHS	Riverside, field and woodland paths, some stretches of road
LANDSCAPE	River estuary, farmland dotted with patches of woodland
SUGGESTED MAP	AA Walker's Map 3 New Forest
START/FINISH	Grid reference: SU483067
DOG FRIENDLINESS	Keep dogs on lead
PARKING	Pay-and-display car park by Quay in Hamble-le-Rice
PUBLIC TOILETS	Hamble-le-Rice
NOTES	The passenger ferry to Warsash runs weekdays 9–4 and weekends 9–5.30

Hamble estuary, between Bursledon and Southampton Water, is one of the longest and busiest in Britain. The river has a long history of human activity from the first Saxon settlers, who used it as a route to the fertile areas inland, to its current status as Britain's premier yachting centre. Today, this stretch of river is filled with yachts and pleasure craft, but between the 14th and early 19th century both Hamble-le-Rice (its formal name) and Bursledon were major centres for naval shipbuilding.

The valley provided a rich supply of timber for warships, the ironworks at nearby Hungerford Bottom supplied essential fastenings and the bend in the river at Bursledon offered the necessary shelter for the Hamble to be ideal for this vital industry. At its peak during the Napoleonic Wars, the Elephant Yard, next to The Jolly Sailor pub, built the 74-gun HMS *Elephant*, Nelson's flagship at the Battle of Copenhagen. Two great local shipbuilders were George Parsons, who built the *Elephant*, and Philemon Ewer. The best-known ship to be built at Hamble was the *Grace Dieu* for Henry V in the 15th century. It was at Hamble Common in 1545 that Henry VIII watched in horror as his flagship, the *Mary Rose*, sank with the loss of 700 men just off the coast.

The six tiny Victory Cottages you pass in Lower Swanwick, near the present-day Moody's Yard, were built in the late 18th century for shipyard workers. The bustling marinas and moorings at Bursledon, best viewed from the terrace of The Jolly Sailor, have only appeared in the last 70 years.

Today, Hamble and Old Bursledon are a delight to explore. Hamble has a twisting main street, lined with pretty Georgian buildings, leading down to the Quay with lovely river views. Old Bursledon has a High Street but no shops, just peaceful lanes dotted with interesting buildings, in particular the timber-framed Dolphin, a former pub.

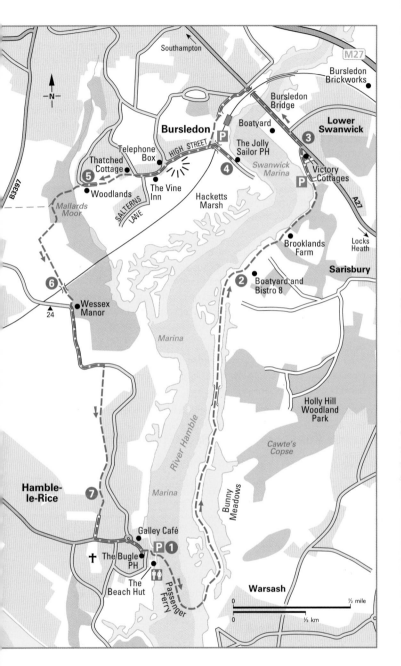

1. From the quayside car park, walk to the pontoon and take the passenger ferry across the estuary to Warsash (weather permitting; for details and fares, visit hambleferry.co.uk). Turn left along the raised gravel path beside the estuary and mudflats and then cross a footbridge and continue to a gravelled parking area.

2. Follow the tarmac path through a boatyard, pass Bistro 8 and turn left, following the painted lines on tarmac and in front of the marina office, and rejoin the riverside path. Go through a kissing gate. Keep ahead at a lane, pass Victory Cottages on your right, and continue to the A27.

3. Turn left, pass Swanwick Marina, and cross Bursledon Bridge. (Turn right before the bridge to visit Bursledon Brickworks.) Pass under the railway, turn left into Church Lane, then fork left into Station Road. Turn left into the station car park, following signs for The Jolly Sailor. Climb a steep path to the road. Turn left at the junction, then left again, and descend steps to the pub.

4. Return along the lane and fork left along the High Street into Old Bursledon. Pause at the viewpoint at Hacketts Marsh, then bear left at the telephone box along the High Street. Pass The Vine Inn and Salterns Lane, then, at a right bend, bear off left by Thatched Cottage (although note that it is not thatched) along a footpath.

5. Join a metalled lane beside the drive to the Coach House then, as the lane curves right, keep ahead beside a house called Woodlands, following the footpath downhill to cross a stream via a footbridge. Proceed uphill through woodland (Mallards Moor). At a junction of paths on the woodland fringe, bear left with the wider bridleway, then at a concrete road bear right, and soon after go left to join a fenced bridleway.

6. Cross a railway bridge and soon reach a road. Keep left round a sharp left-hand bend. Look out for a waymarked footpath on your right, next to an oil pipeline compound, and follow this straight path through a kissing gate and behind houses for 0.5 miles (800m).

7. Join a metalled path and keep ahead past modern housing and a children's play area to a road. Follow Hamble House Gardens out to the High Street and turn left. At the roundabout, bear right down Lower High Street back to the quay and the car park.

Where to eat and drink

There's a range of pubs and tearooms in Hamble, notably the Galley Café, The Beach Hut and The Bugle. Stop off at The Jolly Sailor in Bursledon for good ale or The Vine Inn in Old Bursledon.

What to see

Just before high tide you may see up to 12 species of waders, including dunlin, redshank, lapwing and curlew, and wildfowl – shelduck, teal and brent geese (in winter) – feeding on the mudflats.

While you're there

Visit Bursledon Brickworks. Restored by a trust in 1990, it is the last surviving example of a steam-driven brickworks in the country, with a working steam engine, exhibition on the history and development of brickmaking, hands-on activities and events.

TITCHFIELD'S HISTORIC CANAL

DISTANCE/TIME	7 miles (11.3km) / 2hrs 30min
ASCENT/GRADIENT	220ft (67m) / ▲
PATHS	Canal towpath, clifftop path, tracks and field paths
LANDSCAPE	Nature reserve water-meadows, coastline, open farmland
SUGGESTED MAP	OS Explorer OL3 Meon Valley, Portsmouth, Gosport & Fareham
START/FINISH	Grid reference: SU541054
DOG FRIENDLINESS	Some road walking; otherwise under strict control by nature reserve
PARKING	Bridge Street car park by canal towpath
PUBLIC TOILETS	Meon Shore

Sleepy Titchfield, with its well-preserved village centre and several old pubs, lies surrounded by water-meadows and woods close to the busy A27 and the sprawling suburbs of Fareham. It's hard to imagine today, but Titchfield was an important market town and a busy port in the Middle Ages, thanks to the prosperity of its abbey, founded in 1232, and its position beside the River Meon.

Waterways

By the early 17th century, Titchfield was linked to the sea by a navigable channel, allowing ships to reach the village to trade. The 3rd Earl of Southampton built a dyke at the mouth of the river, and in 1611 a canal was completed as part of an ambitious scheme to close the Meon estuary and replace the tidal channel with a canal. Access from the sea was by a simple lock, and ships had to float in at high tide. Just before reaching Meon Shore on this walk, you will pass what remains of the sea lock. Trade continued coming into Titchfield from the sea as barges travelled up the canal via the sea lock, each vessel being pulled along by horses on the towpath. Although never a success, Titchfield Canal, regarded as the second-oldest artificial waterway in Britain, still exists, and the towpath provides a splendid walk to the coast.

Titchfield Haven Nature Reserve

Building the dyke here turned the saltwater estuary into a freshwater marsh and lush water-meadows, now known as Titchfield Haven. It shelters a rich variety of plants and wildlife, notably marsh marigolds, flowering rushes, wildfowl, waders and summer migrant birds. Take your binoculars and visit Titchfield Haven Nature Reserve. It covers over 300 acres (121ha) of reedbed, freshwater marsh and fen from the coast to Titchfield and hides are accessible to view wintering wildfowl and waders. Permits and visitor facilities are available from Titchfield Haven Visitor Centre.

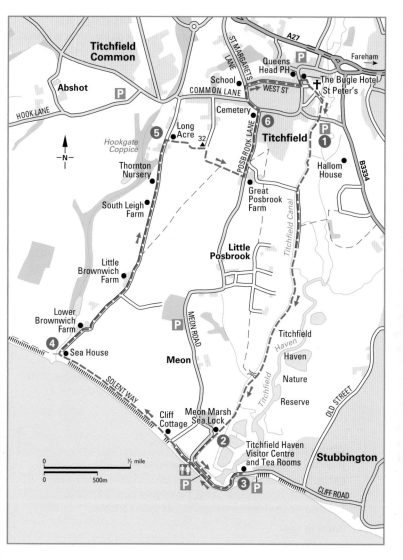

1. From the car park, turn left through the kissing gate onto the towpath, heading south. Continue for about 2 miles (3.2km), with the channel on your right and the nature reserve on your left. After about 0.5 miles (800m) of this stretch, go through a gate, ignoring the gate to your right, and the track becomes tarmac. Pass a bridge and keep ahead. Cross a concrete bridge with sluice gates where the channel diverts, and keep straight on to a kissing gate.

2. Go straight ahead to visit the Meon Marsh Sea Lock, where the road now crosses the canal. Return to the gate and take the footpath on the right, through the trees. Follow the path as it bends left along the shore, just below the road. At the gate, join the road and follow it over the bridge to Titchfield Haven Visitor Centre and café. (You can buy a ticket here if you want to visit the nature reserve itself.)

3. Return along the road and the top of the sea wall. Pass some wooden chalets, and turn left beside a waymarked gate to walk on the gravel between the chalets. At the end, head left, then right and up the path. Follow this path along the cliff top, where dense wind-sculpted hedges give way to spectacular views across the Solent to the Isle of Wight, and ahead to the power station and oil refinery.

4. Follow the path down in front of Sea House to the beach. Follow the signed path immediately right, inland, beside a barrier. Stay on this track, bearing right after the gate at Lower Brownwich Farm onto concrete. Keep to the drive to reach a fork. Keep ahead, following the yellow waymarker, past the cottages and barns of Little Brownwich Farm on the left. Concrete becomes an earth track. Stay on this for 0.5 miles (800m), passing South Leigh Farm on the left.

5. Go through a gateway and turn immediately right through a kissing gate onto a permissive path. Follow this along a left-hand field edge, with Portsmouth's Spinnaker Tower ahead on the horizon. On reaching a track, turn left through a kissing gate, then right at the fork, and continue down the drive, going through a kissing gate to reach Posbrook Lane. Turn left along the footpath and follow this for 0.25 miles (400m) into Titchfield, passing Posbrook Lane cemetery.

6. At the T-junction turn left, then right into St Margarets Lane. Turn right opposite the school, and walk down West Street into the village square. Turn left to explore and walk clockwise around The Square. Turn left beside the Co-op supermarket into Church Street and walk up to St Peter's church. Bear right beside the graveyard, keep ahead and cross a footbridge over the canal. Turn right along the towpath and follow it to Bridge Street. Cross over to return to the car park.

Where to eat and drink

There are several pubs in Titchfield. The Bugle Hotel in The Square and the Queens Head in the High Street are both close to the route, and The Wheatsheaf in East Street serves good food. The café at Titchfield Haven visitor centre also serves snacks and teas.

What to see

Take a closer look at St Peter's church in Titchfield. It may be the oldest in Hampshire and contains a fine tomb to the Earls of Southampton. The porch is said to date from the 7th century.

While you're there

Just north of Titchfield are the impressive ruins of Titchfield Abbey. This medieval structure was converted into a fine Tudor mansion in 1537 by Thomas Wriothesley, the first Earl of Southampton. The 3rd Earl is known to have been a patron of William Shakespeare, and it is possible that some of his plays were performed here for the first time. The house was partially demolished in 1781.

AROUND EMSWORTH HARBOUR

DISTANCE/TIME	4.8 miles (7.8km) / 2hrs
ASCENT/GRADIENT	203ft (62m) / ▲
PATHS	Field-edge path, gravel or metalled shoreline paths, and short stretch along pebble foreshore
LANDSCAPE	Foreshore and marshy coastline
SUGGESTED MAP	AA Walker's Map 20 Chichester & The South Downs
START/FINISH	Grid reference: SU749056
DOG FRIENDLINESS	Keep under control at all times
PARKING	Pay-and-display car park in South Street, Emsworth
PUBLIC TOILETS	Emsworth

Situated at the head of one of the tidal creeks of Chichester Harbour, Emsworth is a small seafaring town, with an attractive jumble of streets, lanes and alleys, and a yacht-filled harbour. During the 18th and 19th centuries it was a principal port along this stretch of coast and became extremely prosperous through activities such as corn milling, boat building, fishing and a flourishing oyster industry.

The town still boasts shipwrights and chandleries, and fishing boats still work out of the harbour, but today it is more important as a yachting centre. If you stroll through the streets and by the harbour you can see the old tide mills that milled the grain from local farms, and admire the houses built by wealthy merchants. Savour the views across the harbour, which are best at low tide, especially during the winter months when the mudflats are a haven for thousands of waders and wildfowl, including curlew, redshank, dunlin, shelduck and mallard. Take your binoculars with you on this walk, as birdlife abounds along its length. In winter, at high tide, you may see diving ducks like goldeneye and red-breasted merganser in the harbour, while in the fields you are likely to spot brent geese feeding.

Isolated Warblington

All that remains of Warblington Castle (private) is a tall brick turret visible through the trees. Once an imposing fortified manor house, it was built by the Countess of Salisbury between 1513 and 1526. She was executed at the Tower of London in 1541 on the orders of Henry VIII, because of her disapproval of his marriage to his friend Catherine of Aragon. The isolated church here dates from the 9th century, when there was a monastery on the site, and is well worth closer inspection. The churchyard is full of interesting gravestones, several with fine carvings reflecting tragedies at sea. Note the ancient yew tree on the left as you enter the churchyard, which is estimated to be over 1,500 years old, and measures more than 26ft (8m) round.

Picturesque Langstone

As a result of its position at an important crossing point to Hayling Island and the abundant availability of fresh water from the Lymbourne stream, Langstone grew into a thriving harbour village. You will arrive at its seaward end, a delightful spot favoured by artists, complete with a pub, an old tide mill, windmill and the broad expanse of Langstone Harbour, with its tidal creeks, saltmarsh islands and mudflats. Much of this fragile landscape is now protected by a nature reserve.

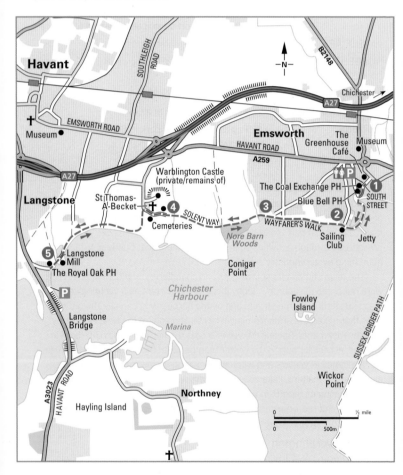

1. Turn right out of the car park and walk down South Street past the Blue Bell pub to the Quay. Keep ahead to join the tarmac path that follows the causeway round the Mill Pond, adjacent to the main harbour. Pass a jetty on the left.

2. Pass beside Emsworth Sailing Club (on your left) and keep straight on to join a concrete path above the shoreline, with houses and gardens to your right. The track broadens into Western Parade. Go through a gap at the end, to stay on the coastal path. Pass a small parking area and continue on the tarmac path, which has become narrow again.

3. The path becomes gravelled as you near a grassy area at the entrance to Nore Barn Woods. Go past a metal barrier and ignore the foreshore path here (impassable at high tides). Keep ahead through the edge of the wood to a junction of paths. Go straight ahead through a kissing gate, ignoring the one to your right, and cross a stream. Beyond another kissing gate, keep to the field-edge towards the ruined tower of Warblington Castle. Pass through three more kissing gates and then between cemeteries to reach a road.

4. Keep ahead through the metal kissing gate into Warblington churchyard. Pass the church on your right to reach the main gate. Turn left on exiting the main gate and turn right into Warblington cemetery. Follow the metalled path round to the left and soon bear right to a kissing gate into pasture. Bear diagonally left to a kissing gate on the harbour shore, and turn right along the sea-wall path. Your path soon drops down onto the foreshore (access may be difficult at exceptionally high tides). In 200yds (183m) rise up off the foreshore and join a metalled path leading past the mill pond, over a small footbridge and then past Langstone mill to reach the former smugglers' haunt, The Royal Oak, on your right.

5. Relax on one of the benches on the seafront and absorb the view across the harbour to Hayling Island before retracing your steps back to Emsworth.

Where to eat and drink

There's a good choice of pubs, restaurants and cafés in Emsworth, notably The Greenhouse Café in The Square for home-made lunches and teas, Flintstones Tearoom on the Quay, and the Blue Bell and Coal Exchange pubs in South Street. The Royal Oak at Langstone is open all day and enjoys great harbour views (dogs welcome).

What to see

Note the two flintstone huts in Warblington churchyard. Built more than 200 years ago, they were designed to house graveyard watchmen in an era when bodies were scarce for medical students to practise on, so were often stolen after recent burials.

While you're there

Stroll through the narrow streets of Emsworth, lined with specialist shops, and explore its history at Emsworth Museum in North Street. Look for the blue plaque on a house in Record Road. The author of the *Jeeves and Wooster* novels, P G Wodehouse, lived here between 1904 and 1913 and based many of his locations and characters on local places and people.

FARLINGTON MARSHES

DISTANCE/TIME	2.5 miles (4km) / 1hr 15min
ASCENT/GRADIENT	52ft (16m) / ▲
PATHS	Mostly gravel tracks but the final grassy section can be muddy, particularly in winter
LANDSCAPE	Grazing marsh, wetlands and harbour wall
SUGGESTED MAP	AA Walker's Map 20 Chichester & The South Downs
START/FINISH	Grid reference: SU680044
DOG FRIENDLINESS	On lead at all times
PARKING	Coastal car park by A27 (may be very busy at weekends)
PUBLIC TOILETS	None on route
NOTES	The harbour wall is very exposed and it can be surprisingly cold at any time of year, so do check the forecast and ensure you bring some warm clothing with you.

Farlington Marshes, just across the Broom Channel from Portsea Island and the teeming city centre, are right in Portsmouth's back garden. Cut off from the north by the busy A27 and surrounded on three sides by Langstone Harbour, this peaceful wildlife reserve has been managed by the Hampshire and Isle of Wight Wildlife Trust since 1962.

Today these low-lying fields are internationally important for wildlife. The grassland areas are bright with butterflies and summer wild flowers, which include rarities such as sea barley, bulbous foxtail and slender hare's-ear. Summer is also the time to see breeding lapwing and skylark, while in winter the fields offer grazing and shelter to thousands of brent geese. Other birds to look out for in and around the lagoons and reedbeds include bearded tits, wigeon, teal and black-tailed godwits.

But the site also has a fascinating history. The marshes as you'll see them now were created in the late 18th century, when the Lord of the Manor of Farlington reclaimed them from Langstone Harbour by linking some of the islands with a clay and timber wall. From that time, the marshes have provided rich grazing meadows and cattle were once raised here.

Wartime deception

This pastoral idyll was rudely disturbed during World War II, when the War Department established an anti-aircraft battery on the site. The marshes were also used as a decoy to draw enemy bombers away from Portsmouth after a heavy raid in January 1941. Fires were lit in specially constructed bunkers, tricking the German pilots into bombing the still waters of Langstone Harbour instead of the blacked-out city centre. Look out for a couple of wartime brick structures as you walk around the harbour wall, as well as some small, round ponds formed in old bomb craters further inland. Another wartime casualty was the oyster watchman's house, built in 1819 on the tiny island that you'll see just across the water as the harbour wall turns north. The house, which belonged to a Matthew Russell, has never been rebuilt, but Russell's Lake still runs south from the island he once called home.

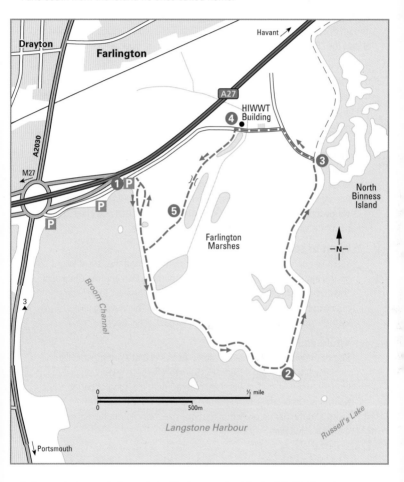

1. Leave the car park through the kissing gate beside the Wildlife Trust's notice boards and walk down the slope to the information board. Turn right through a kissing gate and onto the harbour wall. The winding coastal path offers exceptional views across Langstone Harbour and turns hard left after almost 1 mile (1.6km).

2. The scenery changes as you head north, with views to the red-brick Victorian forts along the top of Portsdown Hill. Continue walking past a viewing area and an information panel, followed by an old wartime bunker, then keep an eye out for the low bulk of North Binness Island drawing closer on your right.

3. Turn left, off the harbour wall just after two gateposts, missing the gate and dropping down to pass through a similar pair of gateposts a few paces further on. Follow the gravel track and after 275yds (251m) turn left at the junction and pass the Wildlife Trust's whitewashed storage building. Continue walking to reach a kissing gate some 100yds (91m) further on.

4. Turn left through the gate and follow the waymarked grassy path (via short white posts on the left of the path) into the heart of the reserve, with reedbeds and an open wetland area on your left. Cross the plank bridge and continue ahead for 200yds (183m), keeping a sizeable lake to your left.

5. Continue on the marked path along a fence on the left to a gate. Pass through a kissing gate and climb the bank, turn right and at a fork in the path bear right, away from the harbour wall and through a kissing gate and rejoin the outward route at the information board just before the car park.

Where to eat and drink

Just 1.5 miles (2.4km) down Eastern Road on Portsea Island, the Great Salterns Harvester offers unlimited salad with its range of grills, burgers and family favourites. Turn the corner into Burrfields Road for sandwiches, baguettes and jacket potatoes, as well as pub classics and big plate specials at the Farmhouse Hungry Horse.

What to see

You'll get outstanding views across Portsmouth and the Isle of Wight on the early stages of your walk. Taller than Big Ben and the Blackpool Tower, the distinctive 558ft (170m) Emirates Spinnaker Tower stands guard over the waterfront at Gunwharf Quays. The viewing decks include a chance to walk on Europe's largest glass floor.

While you're there

Eight hundred years of naval history awaits you at Portsmouth Historic Dockyard. Visit Nelson's iconic HMS *Victory* and HMS *Warrior*, the world's first iron-hulled warship, in an authentic setting of period naval buildings. Other attractions include the *Mary Rose* museum, harbour tours and the hands-on Action Stations experience. Site tickets are valid for a full year.

PORTSMOUTH HARBOUR AND HISTORIC DOCKYARD

DISTANCE/TIME	3.5 miles (5.6km) / 2hrs
ASCENT/GRADIENT	102ft (31m) / ▲
PATHS	Sea wall defences, cobbled streets and pavements
LANDSCAPE	Historic streets, docklands, busy harbour and waterfront
SUGGESTED MAP	AA Walker's Map 16 Isle of Wight
START/FINISH	Grid reference: SZ634990
DOG FRIENDLINESS	Not suitable for dogs
PARKING	Pay-and-display at Clarence Pier car park (right of Amusement Park)
PUBLIC TOILETS	White Hart Road, Gunwharf Quays and the Hard

Portsmouth has been the home of the Royal Navy for more than 800 years, playing a key role in the defence of the British Empire and synonymous with Nelson's victory at Trafalgar (1805). It was from here that many of Britain's naval heroes set sail, and their legacy lives on in Old Portsmouth, with its quaint houses, colourful waterfront and historic dockyard. Walk along the fortifications, through the cobbled streets of Spice Island, and discover Britain's naval heritage by touring the dockyard, museums and exhibitions.

Spice Island, a tiny peninsula of narrow cobbled lanes, lay outside the 17th-century walls and during the 18th and 19th centuries was bursting with all the life, danger and excitement one associates with a thriving naval port. At one time, it was said, 2,000 prostitutes and 200 beer houses could be found here, along with gambling saloons and cockfighting. The oldest house in Old Portsmouth, Quebec House (1754), was originally built by public subscription as a seawater bathing house. Founded in 1212 as a hospice for travellers and the sick, the Garrison Church was where Charles II married his Portuguese bride, Catherine of Braganza, in 1662. The waterfront land, closed to the public for centuries, has now been opened up for everyone to enjoy. There are public promenades, viewing terraces for maritime events and berths for tall ships, and the bright and bustling Gunwharf Quays complex now features cafés, bars, restaurants, a 14-screen cinema and more than 90 shops.

Allow plenty of time to visit the Naval Dockyard, for there is much to see and explore. See the spot where Nelson died on HMS *Victory*, view the hull of Henry VIII's favourite warship, the *Mary Rose*, which sank in 1545 with the loss of 700 men and dramatically rose from the seabed in 1982, then step back in time and experience life aboard a Tudor warship by visiting the amazing *Mary Rose* exhibition. Explore the four vast decks of HMS *Warrior*, Britain's first ironclad battleship, built in 1860, and discover more about the Navy in the absorbing Royal Navy Museum.

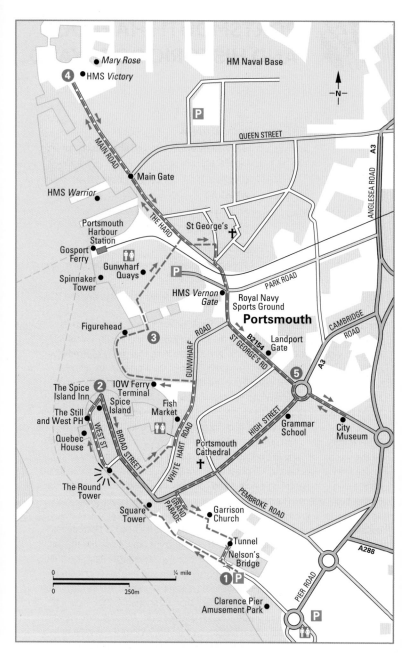

1. From the car park, join the Millennium Promenade (Renaissance Trail) and cross the wooden footbridge. Follow the chainlink trail (marked on the paving) along the sea wall, walking away from Clarence Pier. Continue along the wall to the restored Square Tower and proceed to The Round Tower, both built during the 15th century to protect the dockyard. Walk through the tower and

follow the chainlink paving down the steps onto Tower Street and into West Street, passing white weatherboarded Quebec House, to The Still and West pub and the Point, the heart of Spice Island.

2. Curve right, following the chainlink along Broad Street, then left along Feltham Row, passing between the old fishing harbour and new housing developments to White Hart Road. Turn left, pass the Fish Market and continue ahead along Gunwharf Road, passing the Isle of Wight ferry terminal. Follow the chainlink left towards the terminal building, then turn right through an ornate metal gate. Follow the chainlink through a development of modern apartment blocks, passing the *HMS Marlborough* figurehead, and into the Gunwharf Quays shopping complex.

3. Follow the trail across the lock, then turn right down Vernon Avenue to reach Central Square. Continue ahead down Marlborough Avenue and pass under the railway and turn left to The Hard beyond Portsmouth Harbour station. Turn left to the Naval Dockyard and Flagship Portsmouth.

4. Return along The Hard, down the short Ordnance Row to St George's church, then bear right to go under the railway and keep ahead along St George's Road, with the sports field on your left. Bear left at the junction with Gunwharf Road to the roundabout.

5. Continue ahead if you want to visit Portsmouth City Museum; otherwise, at the roundabout, turn right along High Street to the cathedral. Turn left into Grand Parade and join the path past Garrison Church. Walk through the tunnel across Nelson's Bridge to return to the car park.

Where to eat and drink

There's a wide choice of pubs and cafés, including the Spice Island and The Still and West in Old Portsmouth. There are also waterfront bars and eating places at Gunwharf Quays and at many of the attractions on the walk's route.

What to see

At the junction of St George's and Park, look for the entrance gates to the former *HMS Vernon*, the long-running site of Royal Navy torpedo and mine clearance diving operations. Along St George's Road, you will pass the Landport Gate, the former principal entrance into the fortified town of Portsmouth.

While you're there

Enjoy a leisurely 50-minute cruise around Portsmouth Harbour and view the warships and fortifications, including Portchester Castle. Visit the 558ft (170m)-tall Emirates Spinnaker Tower in the Gunwharf Quays complex, providing 360-degree views of Portsmouth and Langstone, and over to the Isle of Wight. Visit 393 Commercial Road, the birthplace of Charles Dickens, now a museum.

BEAULIEU TO BUCKLERS HARD

DISTANCE/TIME	4.8 miles (7.7km) / 2hrs 30min
ASCENT/GRADIENT	266ft (81m) / ▲
PATHS	Woodland and riverside paths, gravel track
LANDSCAPE	River valley with woodland, farmland and marshes
SUGGESTED MAP	AA Walker's Map 3 New Forest
START/FINISH	Grid reference: SU386021
DOG FRIENDLINESS	Let them off lead on woodland paths but keep on lead where signs indicate
PARKING	Pay-and-display car park in Beaulieu village
PUBLIC TOILETS	Beaulieu and Bucklers Hard

Set at the head of the Beaulieu River, historic Beaulieu is an attractive village of red-brick Georgian cottages dominated by Palace House, originally the great gatehouse to a Cistercian abbey founded in 1204 by King John. To many visitors, 'Beaulieu' simply means the abbey ruins and the motor museum, but the village itself remains relatively unspoilt and is well worth exploring, with specialist little shops, a fine art gallery, and the ubiquitous semi-wild New Forest ponies and donkeys wandering through and holding up the traffic.

Bucklers Hard

This hamlet, with its single picturesque street leading down to the river, was laid out in the 18th century by the 2nd Duke of Montagu. Having been granted the West Indian islands of St Lucia and St Vincent, he planned to develop a port on the Beaulieu River to import and refine sugar grown on the islands. His dream was shattered when the French invaded his islands. Twenty years later, he inherited the right to a free harbour and, with plentiful timber supplies close by, Bucklers Hard became a prosperous shipbuilding centre. Many wooden warships, including Nelson's *HMS Agamemnon,* were made from New Forest oak here until around 1820. In its busy days the wide main street was used for rolling great logs to the 'hard' where the ships were built. Today, the village is a living museum, the street is free of traffic and looks much as it was in its shipbuilding heyday. You can visit the fascinating Maritime Museum and learn about the shipbuilding industry, then explore authentically reconstructed cottage and inn interiors to gain an insight into the life of the workers in the 18th century, before strolling along the riverbank to view the remains of the inlets where some of the 50 wooden naval and merchant vessels were built.

Bailey's Hard

About halfway between Beaulieu and Bucklers Hard is a cluster of cottages, and a house with an industrial-scale chimney. This is Bailey's Hard, the site of a thriving brick-making industry in the 18th century. Bricks were made here until the 1930s, and many were used in the estate houses. They were shipped downriver and along the coast to Southampton. This is also where the first naval vessel to be built on the Beaulieu River, the *Salisbury*, was completed in 1698, before the industry moved downstream. Much of the walking route passes through woodland once used for shipbuilding. Keeping Copse was replanted in about 1820, after much of the mature timber had been felled for this purpose. You can still identify some of the trees that were encouraged to grow the heavy side branches used in the ship's frames.

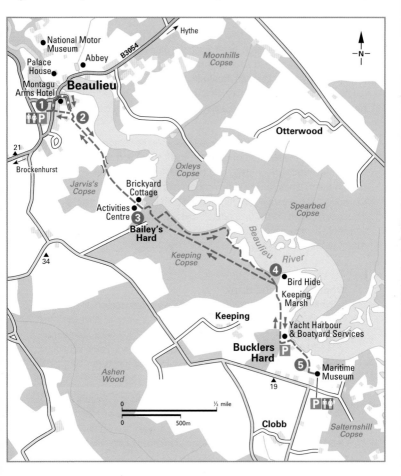

1. Take the gravel track to the side of the car park entrance past the Old Bakehouse Tearooms to the High Street. Turn left and follow it down to the main road. Turn right, passing the front of the handsome Montagu Arms Hotel, and turn immediately right along the tarmac road beside the hotel. This becomes a gravel track near the fire station. Stay on this as it goes round the back of the hotel and past the hotel car parks, to bear left through a gate.

2. Follow the broad gravel track between meadows, passing through a gate, through the strip of Jarvis's Copse, and along the side of a field to pass a gate beside Brickyard Cottage, at Bailey's Hard. Continue along the track through

woodland. Shortly, bear right then left along the track, signed to 'Bucklers Hard and Solent Way', beside a wooden barrier.

3. After 200yds (183m) head off left on the Riverside Walk, signed to 'Bucklers Hard'. Cross a footbridge and follow the winding path through the trees and along boardwalks, enjoying the views to the river. Where the path almost meets the inland track, keep left over a bridge. Cross two footbridges and bear round to the right. Cross another four footbridges and when, at the fourth, the path almost meets the track, keep left.

4. At a seat overlooking the river the path bends inland to a small car park. Rejoin the main gravel track, go through the gate ahead and follow the track right past the entrance to a birding hide at Keeping Marsh. Stay on the track to pass the boatyard on your left. Bear left at the entrance to the boatyard, and follow the signposted route past a car park and down to the water's edge. Turn right to pass the thatched Duke's Bath House, and continue to the quay in Bucklers Hard.

5. Turn right up the broad main street to explore the village. The museum and tearoom are at the top. Return down the main street and turn left along the riverbank, retracing your steps past the boatyard. This time, keep left, just beyond the bird hide, past a gate for the direct route back to Beaulieu through the woods. At the gate at Point 2, take the path left through a gate, signed 'Beaulieu Village'. Follow the path left and right round the school playing field and between houses to emerge on the High Street. Cross straight over to return to the car park.

Where to eat and drink

In Bucklers Hard you will find the Captain's Cabin tearoom and the Master Builder's House Hotel (Yachtsman's Bar open all day), the latter offering good bar food. In Beaulieu, try the Old Bakehouse Tearooms, or Monty's for real ale and pub food. Steff's Kitchen in Fairweather's Garden Centre also serves very good snacks and lunches.

What to see

As you walk beside the Beaulieu River look out for the waders and wildfowl, including shelduck, curlew, redshank and oystercatcher, that thrive on the tidal mudflats and salt marsh. Make a point of visiting Beaulieu Abbey church (free access before noon), formerly the monks refectory. Note the original 13th-century stone pulpit, reached via a vaulted staircase, and the graves of Lady Isabella, wife of King John's son, the Earl of Cornwall, who died in 1240, and that of Princess Eleana, infant daughter of Edward I.

While you're there

Take a cruise on the tranquil Beaulieu River from Bucklers Hard and view the abundant birdlife on the salt marshes. On your return to Beaulieu, visit Palace House, home of Lord Montagu, and the adjacent remains of the 13th-century abbey with its exhibition on monastic life. If time allows, take a look at the famous National Motor Museum.

EXBURY GARDENS AND LEPE COUNTRY PARK

DISTANCE/TIME	6.6 miles (10.7km) / 3hrs
ASCENT/GRADIENT	335ft (102m) / ▲
PATHS	Fields, woodland and foreshore paths, some roads, 3 stiles
LANDSCAPE	Coastline and farmland dotted with woodland
SUGGESTED MAP	AA Walker's Map 3 New Forest
START/FINISH	Grid reference: SZ455985
DOG FRIENDLINESS	Keep dogs under control at all times
PARKING	ANPR (pay on exit) car park at Lepe Country Park
PUBLIC TOILETS	Lepe Country Park

With its shingle beaches, wild natural habitats and clumps of pine trees, Lepe Country Park is a perfect place to begin exploring one of the remote and most beautiful stretches of the Hampshire coast. It affords superb views across the Solent to the Isle of Wight and provides an excellent vantage point to watch passing yachts and ships, in particular huge tankers making their way to the oil refinery at nearby Fawley. To the west lie silent and eerie mudflats and marshland expanses at the mouth of the Beaulieu River and the fine gardens at Exbury, the focus of this walk.

Outstanding gardens

Exbury is a rare surviving example of an estate village and enjoys an enviable position, being peacefully situated on the edge of the New Forest and just a mile (1.6km) from the Solent coast. Pride of place in the village goes to Exbury House and its 200 acres (81ha) of landscaped woodland gardens which lie on the sheltered east bank of the beautiful Beaulieu River. The gardens were the life's work of Lionel de Rothschild, a member of the banking family, who bought the estate in 1919. Having extended the early 19th-century house he set to work establishing one of the most outstanding rhododendron gardens in the world.

The acid-rich soil already supported fine specimens of oak, great cedars and Wellingtonias, which provided the perfect backdrop for the rhododendrons and other acid-loving plants, including azaleas, camellias and magnolias. Today, the gardens are internationally famous for rhododendrons and azaleas and over 1,200 hybrids have been created. A network of tracks enables you to explore the countless plantings, the cascades and ponds, a rose garden, heather garden and iris garden, daffodil meadow and a delightful walk along the banks of the river with views across to Bucklers Hard.

Exbury provides a feast of visual delights all year round and you should allow at least two hours for a visit, especially in the spring and autumn. Stroll through the gardens in late spring and the vibrant colours of the rhododendrons and azaleas will be mesmerising. On a warm June day, head for the rose garden to experience the amazing range and the intoxicating scent of hundreds of blooms, while high summer is the perfect time to relax in the shade of the great trees, including ancient, awe-inspiring yews, and admire the peace and beauty of Exbury. Come here in the autumn and the beautiful specimen trees will reward you with a magnificent display of purples, bronzes and mellow brown colours.

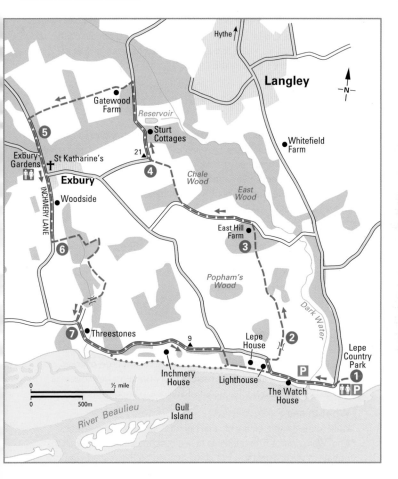

1. Walk west from the shore car park along the road. Keep left along the path above the foreshore, and pass the Watch House. Then, at a small white light-house, turn right, going up the slope to meet the lane. Turn left then, as the road curves left, go through a kissing gate on the right. Walk along the field edge then bear left through a gate and over a bridge.

2. Keep alongside the fence to a kissing gate and proceed straight across the field. Briefly pass beside some woodland and follow the path to a gap in the hedge near a telegraph pole. Follow the path across the next large field and into the woodland ahead. Continue through the trees, bearing right after

crossing a footbridge, then right with a waymarker post to join a fenced bridle-way arrowed to the left.

3. Pass East Hill Farm and walk along the gravelled farm track until it curves sharp left. Turn right through a gate. Bear left following the wide path between hedges, and then on entering a field follow the right-hand field edge to a T-junction. Turn left to a stile and lane.

4. Turn right, continue through a gate beside a cattle grid and take the footpath left through a gate (by another cattle grid) to join a track to Gatewood Farm. Bear right at the fork, walk around the farm complex, and remain on the track for 0.75 miles (1.2km) to a gate and lane. Go straight across for Exbury Gardens (where there's a tearoom).

5. On leaving Exbury Gardens, turn right along the road, then, where the road bends left, keep ahead, signed 'Inchmery Lane'. Continue to a waymarked path and stile on the left.

6. Cross the stile and walk straight across grassland into woodland, following the path right, through the trees, crossing over a plank bridge with a pond on the right. On leaving the trees, turn right along the field edge beside the wood-land to a gap in the hedge near a three-way signpost. Keep the woodland edge on your right until the path bears right over a footbridge into woods. Two more footbridges lead out via a kissing gate to a lane.

7. Turn left, along the lane and follow it around Inchmery House then, just before the road junction, turn right beside a barrier down to the foreshore to pick up the path towards Lepe House. If the tide is out the alternative route is along the foreshore. Pass Lepe House and rejoin your outward route past The Watch House back to Lepe Country Park.

Where to eat and drink
Lepe Country Park has a seasonal restaurant and refreshment kiosk. There's also a licensed restaurant, with no access charge, offering coffee, good light lunches and teas at Exbury Gardens. Delicious teas can be had at Mr Eddy's Tea Rooms if you're exploring Exbury.

What to see
Walk to the eastern extent of Lepe Country Park to see some relics from World War II. The extensive raised concrete platforms are all that remain of the construction site of the floating 'Mulberry' harbours that were towed across to Normandy for the D-Day landings in June 1944.

While you're there
Visit Calshot Castle. Down past the oil refineries and power stations east of Lepe you will find this Tudor fort, built for Henry VIII on the spit beyond the tidal flats of Southampton Water. There are excellent Solent views and the former flying boat base is now home to an outdoor pursuits centre.

KEYHAVEN AND THE SOLENT

DISTANCE/TIME	5.4 miles (8.7km) / 2hrs
ASCENT/GRADIENT	118ft (36m) / ▲
PATHS	Sea-wall path, tracks and short stretch of road
LANDSCAPE	Salt and freshwater marshland
SUGGESTED MAP	AA Walker's Map 3 New Forest
START/FINISH	Grid reference: SZ306914
DOG FRIENDLINESS	Strict control needed around nature reserve
PARKING	Pay-and-display car park in Keyhaven (arrive early on summer days)
PUBLIC TOILETS	Keyhaven car park

Between Hurst Spit at the western end of the Solent and the ancient town of Lymington lies a huge expanse of salt and freshwater marshes and mudflats, a breezy, watery landscape that's more reminiscent perhaps of East Anglia than Hampshire. The area is a birder's paradise, with the marshes, lagoons and ponds attracting rare and interesting species, especially in the winter, so take your binoculars on this walk. From your vantage point on the sea wall you can scan the saltings and pools and see a wide range of waders and wildfowl. Sightings could include a heron loping lazily across a lagoon, a curlew probing the mud with its long, down-curved bill, shelduck in the shallows, and skylarks singing high above the reedbeds. Walk this way in winter and you should see flocks of black-necked brent geese feeding on the eelgrass, long-tailed ducks, greenshanks and, out on the Solent, goldeneye and common scoter. The elegant common and sandwich terns, which breed on Hurst Spit, can be seen overhead during the summer months and, if you're lucky, you may spot one of the rarer passage migrants, perhaps ruff, curlew sandpiper or little stint.

A salty tale

The area has not always been a refuge for wildlife. Between the 12th and 19th centuries salt extraction was a flourishing industry along this stretch of coastline. At one time there were 13 saltworks on Keyhaven and Pennington marshes. Seawater was impounded in shallow tidal ponds, or 'salterns', about 20ft (6m) square, and left to evaporate. Once it had formed a strong brine, it was pumped by wind pump into boiling houses with coal-fired furnaces, where it was boiled until salt crystals were left. Lymington salt was highly regarded and by the 18th century supplied much of southern England and was even exported to America. In 1800, 4,000 tons were produced, but when new railways brought in cheaper rock salt from Cheshire the industry declined. You can see the remains of the old salt pans' square enclosures from the sea wall at Oxey Marsh. The Chequers Inn at Pennington is closely linked with the salt industry. As well as being well placed to serve thirsty salt workers, it was where the outgoing salt was checked for tax purposes, hence its name.

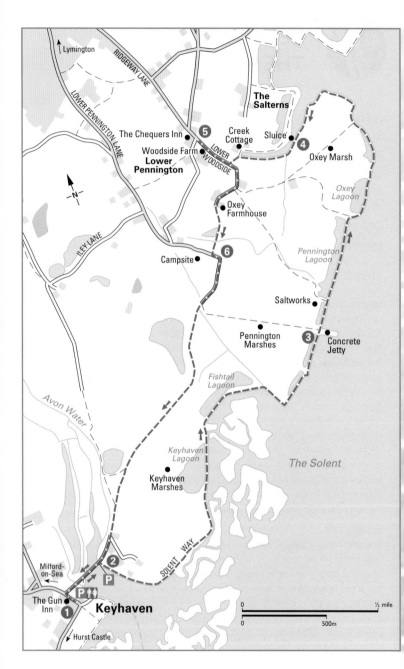

1. With The Gun Inn behind you, take the footpath ahead on the opposite side of the car park, following green Solent Way arrows. Turn right, with the harbour on your right. Cross a bridge and turn right through a gate beyond the parking area, signed running and walking trails.

2. Remain on the good shingle path close to the foreshore, then continue along the sea wall, with fine views across the Solent to The Needles and Tennyson Down on the Isle of Wight and Hurst Castle on the mainland. Inland views take in the wildlife-rich Keyhaven Marshes. Continue through a gate beside Keyhaven Lagoon, enjoying the birdlife on both sides of the route. Pass Fishtail Lagoon, and reach a concrete jetty, a relic from World War II, when so much of this southern shore played a part in the preparations for D-Day and the Normandy landings.

3. Ignore all paths inland, but stay on the sea-wall path to skirt Pennington Lagoon and then Oxey Lagoon, with Oxey Marsh behind. Follow the coast inland, with distant views of a forest of masts at Lymington Marina, before heading southwest beside a channel to an old sluice gate.

4. Ignoring the path right, over the sluice, keep ahead down four steps. After 120yds (110m) turn right through a gate and head towards Creek Cottage on a narrow path beside the creek. The two old brick buildings you can see across the creek were salt boiling houses. Shallowdraught lighters brought coal up the creek, known as Moses Dock, for the furnaces and returned loaded with salt. Just before a squeeze stile, bear left and continue to a road, Lower Woodside. Turn right here to visit The Chequers Inn.

5. Retrace your steps and follow Lower Woodside to its end by Oxey Farmhouse. Keep ahead along the footpath to join another road and turn left.

6. Follow it round a sharp right bend and walk beside Pennington Marshes, with a campsite on the right. Where the lane ends, go ahead by a gate. Follow the track through the old saltings and beside Keyhaven Marshes, through a gate onto a road. Follow this to the harbour wall in Keyhaven, retracing your steps from Point 2 back to the car park.

Where to eat and drink
The Chequers Inn, formerly the local salt exchange, dates from the 16th century, has a pleasant, sheltered terrace and garden, and offers a good snack menu and more imaginative dishes. The Gun Inn at Keyhaven is ideally placed by the car park for post-walk refreshments.

What to see
Next door to The Gun Inn in Keyhaven stands Hawkers Cottage, built by the famous wildfowler Peter Hawker in the early 19th century. He kept a diary detailing 50 years of hunting on the marshes.

While you're there
Visit Hurst Castle. Between April and October, you can take the ferry or walk along the pebble beach to Henry VIII's fortress. Completed in 1544 to defend the Solent's western entrance, it was used to imprison Charles I in 1648 and housed coastal gun batteries and searchlights during World War II.

SHALFLEET AND NEWTOWN ESTUARY

DISTANCE/TIME	3.7 miles (5.6km) / 2hrs
ASCENT/GRADIENT	194ft (59m) / ▲
PATHS	Tracks, field paths, raised dykes and some roads, 2 stiles
LANDSCAPE	Gently rolling farmland, woodland and salt marsh
SUGGESTED MAP	AA Walker's Map 16 Isle of Wight
START/FINISH	Grid reference: SZ413894
DOG FRIENDLINESS	Keep dogs under control
PARKING	Roadside off A3054 or on Mill Road
PUBLIC TOILETS	National Trust toilets in Old Town Hall car park; donation appreciated

The Isle of Wight village of Shalfleet developed where the Caul Bourne widens into a creek at the head of the Newtown Estuary. Take a look at the church on the other side of the A3054, with its impressive, fort-like tower, built in the 11th century with 5ft (1.5m)-thick walls and used as a refuge from French invaders during the 14th century, and stroll out to the small 17th-century quay, once busy with boats unloading coal or taking on corn and now popular with yachts and sailing dinghies.

Newtown

The most ancient of the island boroughs, Francheville, as Newtown was once known, was the island's capital, being laid out by the Bishop of Winchester in 1256. Situated on the Newtown River estuary, it developed into a major seaport, with great, masted ships dwarfing bustling quays and trade thriving with local salt and oysters. Its streets were designed on a grid system and their names (Gold Street, Drapers Alley) recall the medieval merchants and craftsmen, although most are now only grassy lanes. Fortunes changed in 1377 when the town was burnt down during a combined French and Spanish raid. It was never fully rebuilt, although the town hall was rebuilt in 1699, and until 1832 it returned two Members of Parliament. Today Newtown, which has no through traffic, is a tranquil place best explored on foot. You can wander along a network of footpaths through the old streets and visit the beautifully restored Victorian church, and the isolated Old Town Hall where you can learn more about the history of this fascinating place.

The marshes

Perhaps surprisingly, the windswept salt marshes and mudflats were only created in their present form as late as 1954, following a violent winter storm which breached the sea wall. Bordering shallow creeks and the estuary, it is a magical place, and a paradise for both birds and birders. Wildfowl and waders abound here. Oystercatchers and redshanks probe the mudflats for morsels, a variety of ducks dabble in the shallows, nesting gulls squabble on Gull Island, and common and little terns glide through the summer air, flocks of geese wheel overhead in winter, and always and everywhere you can hear the bubbling call of the curlew.

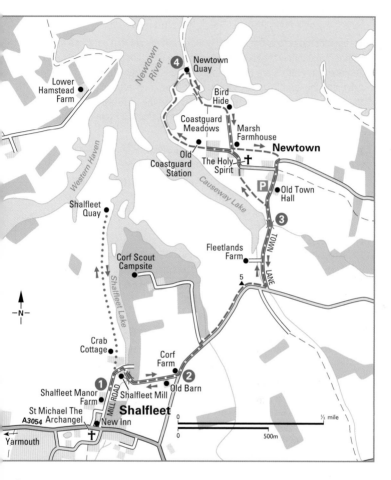

1. Park on roadside beyond The New Inn and walk up Mill Road, then turn right at the fork to pass Shalfleet Mill. Cross the footbridge and follow the path up through woodland, swinging right and then left. Bear left and follow the drive to a road.

2. Turn left past Corf Farm and keep to the road for 200yds (183m) just beyond the entrance to the scout campsite to a kissing gate and permissive path on your left. Keep to the right-hand edge of two fields, parallel with the road, to a kissing gate. Turn left, then left again, along Town Lane, signed to Newtown.

3. Cross the bridge at the head of Causeway Lake and take the path left (public footpath CB16a), towards Newtown village. Walk along the edge of the tidal creek to a gate, then along the lower edge of Hay Meadow. In the second field bear right up the slope to a gate and then join a tree-lined path leading into

Newtown. At the lane, turn right to visit the church of 1837. Retrace your steps and follow the road round to the right. Keep ahead to pass a parking area at the end. Take the path through a gate beside the Old Coastguard Station, signed 'To the Harbour'. Beyond a further gate, keep to the left-hand edge of the meadow to a gate and follow the raised path alongside the estuary. Continue to the black-painted shed at Newtown Quay.

4. Head inland across the narrow wooden boardwalk to a gate. In a few paces turn left and follow the footpath towards the bird hide (run by local experts in summer but visitors are welcome). Bear right at a gate, heading inland to a drive and the lane. Turn left, cross the stile on your left and proceed behind the houses to a stile and lane. Turn right, pass the Old Town Hall and follow the lane down to the bridge at Causeway Lake, Point 3. From here retrace your steps back to Shalfleet Mill and your car.

Extending the walk An enjoyable 1.25 miles (2km) can be added by following the footpath you'll see at the fork in Mill Road. Walk along the unmade track (S12) parallel with the tidal Shalfleet Lake to the boatyard at Shalfleet Quay for a different view of Newtown River and its tidal creeks.

Where to eat and drink

The welcoming, 18th-century New Inn at Shalfleet boasts flagstoned floors, a huge open fireplace, scrubbed pine tables, a good range of ales and an interesting menu that specialises in fresh local fish. There's also a sheltered rear garden.

What to see

Note the finely painted board or inn sign, featuring the arms of the former borough, above the doorway to a fine stone house called Noah's Ark in Newtown. Formerly the village inn, it is the village's oldest surviving building and surrendered its licence in 1916.

While you're there

Visit Newtown Old Town Hall. This small brick-and-stone building was built in the 17th century and stands as a monument to Newtown's past eminence. It houses an exhibition depicting the famous Ferguson's Gang, which restored the building before giving it to the National Trust, and a copy of ancient documents of this notorious 'rotten borough'.

A WOODLAND WALK AT WOOTTON BRIDGE

43

DISTANCE/TIME	3.3 miles (5.3km) / 1hr 20min
ASCENT/GRADIENT	334ft (105m) / ▲ ▲
PATHS	Mostly gravel and surfaced tracks with a short cross-field section, 2 stiles
LANDSCAPE	Rolling wooded farmland
SUGGESTED MAP	AA Walker's Map 16 Isle of Wight
START/FINISH	Grid reference: SZ543919
DOG FRIENDLINESS	Lead required across the fields between Woodhouse and Little Mousehill farms
PARKING	Pay-and-display car park in Brannon Way
PUBLIC TOILETS	Next to the car park

Dividing Wootton Creek from the placid waters of the old Mill Pond, Wootton Bridge is a charming spot. Your route leads quickly away from the bustling main street, passing through farmland and quiet woodlands that are numbered among England's finest wildlife sites.

You'll pass through Hurst Copse soon after leaving the village. Parts of the copse have been planted since the area was mapped in 1793, but the remainder of these ancient woods is probably more than 400 years old and could even date from the end of the last Ice Age. Ash and English oak flourish on the rich soils running down to the Mill Pond and give shade to the lower growing hazel and field maple coppice. The woods, which also support red squirrels, dormice and eight species of bats, are protected under both UK and European wildlife laws.

A railway worth preserving

As you leave the woods behind, you may hear the sound of a steam whistle heralding your first crossing of the Isle of Wight Steam Railway. Originally opened in 1875 as the Ryde and Newport Railway, there were intermediate stations serving the local communities at Wootton and Havenstreet, while the relatively isolated station at Whippingham served Queen Victoria's country house at Osborne. The equally grand but even more remote station at Ashey was probably built as a sweetener for Sir Henry Oglander of Nunwell House, who objected to the railway cutting through his pheasant shoot. A short branch line from Ashey also connected with the local chalk quarry until its closure in 1907, after which trains were left on the branch to serve as a grandstand for the adjacent racecourse.

Following nationalisation in 1948 the little railway was closed in 1966. But the old railway wasn't finished yet. Several locomotives and carriages were preserved and in 1971 the Isle of Wight Steam Railway reopened the section between Wootton and Havenstreet. Twenty years later, the heritage line was extended to Smallbrook Junction and the railway is busier than ever.

150

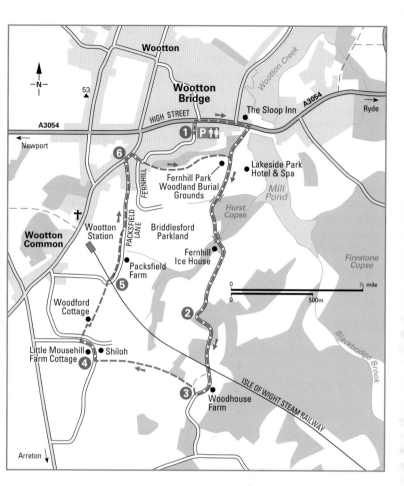

1. Leave the car park and turn right into Brannon Way, then go right down the hill as far as the old Mill Pond. Turn right along public bridleway N1, fork right after 100yds (91m) and then left onto a gravel track at Fernhill Park Woodland Burial Grounds. Go through the gate, follow the track past Hurst Copse and the old ice house on the right, and then go past Briddlesford Parkland, continuing straight ahead.

2. Walk through the shallow valley and climb to the railway level crossing. Keep ahead on N1 for 175yds (160m) through a gate, then bear right past the entrance to Woodhouse Farm and continue for a few more paces, until the track bends left.

3. Turn right through a kissing gate onto public footpath N2. Bear left beside the hedge, through a kissing gate, and follow the tree-shaded path to a stile. Keep ahead across the open field, heading towards a house, then go over the stile and bear slightly left across the next field. Keep ahead after a kissing gate, walking parallel with the hedge on your left to reach bridleway N3 at a final kissing gate.

4. Turn right onto public footpath N3, pass Little Mousehill Farm Cottage and follow the bridleway left at Shiloh. After 100yds (91m) turn right on a public bridleway heading to Woodford Cottage, then zig-zag right and left around the cream-washed cottage onto an attractive hedged path. Drop gently downhill, shaded by oak trees, to reach the railway.

5. Go over the level crossing and turn left at the entrance to Packsfield Farmhouse onto an enclosed path, parallel with the driveway. Ignore all turnings and keep ahead as the path widens into an unmade residential lane to reach a T-junction.

6. Turn right then right again into Fernhill. Keep ahead into Fernside Way, then fork right onto cycle route 22 when the road bears left. Follow the well-surfaced cycle track to the turning area and wooden sculpture at Fernhill Park Woodland Burial Grounds and keep ahead down the drive. Bear left at the gate and walk back to the A3054 opposite The Sloop Inn. Now turn left and retrace your steps to the car park.

Where to eat and drink

Beautifully located with a garden overlooking Wootton Creek, The Sloop Inn is a busy all-day enterprise that nevertheless manages to retain some character and a cosy atmosphere. It serves pizzas, burgers, pub classics, baguettes and wraps and also has a daily carvery, all very good value.

What to see

The ice house that you'll see on the right after passing Briddlesford Parkland was built to serve nearby Fernhill House in the late 18th century. Similar structures were common at great houses before modern refrigeration as a way of preserving winter ice for use in the kitchen throughout the year and about 15 of them still survive on the Isle of Wight.

While you're there

The mill pond on Wootton Creek is formed by a sluice gate in the bridge. At one time there was a second sluice gate in the bridge that would use the tidal water from the mill pond to power a flour mill. The mill was demolished in 1962 and the area later redeveloped for housing, ending 800 years of milling activities in that location.

BEMBRIDGE AND CULVER DOWN

DISTANCE/TIME	5.8 miles (9.3km) / 2hrs 30min
ASCENT/GRADIENT	768ft (234m) / ▲ ▲
PATHS	Coastal and field paths, some road, 3 stiles
LANDSCAPE	Coastal cliffs, pebble beach (sand at low tide) and chalk downland
SUGGESTED MAP	AA Walker's Map 16 Isle of Wight
START/FINISH	Grid reference: SZ657880
DOG FRIENDLINESS	Keep dogs under control; can run free on Culver Down
PARKING	Pay-and-display car park in Bembridge
PUBLIC TOILETS	Beside car park at the start and near the Pilot Boat Inn

Bembridge is almost a place apart on the island's most easterly headland. Formerly a rough fishing and smuggling hamlet, almost cut off by the estuary of the River Yar, it was transformed by land reclamation in the mid-19th century, when a few wealthy Victorians turned it into a fashionable resort with hotels and holiday villas in their own grounds. Brading Marshes stretch behind the village, the first RSPB nature reserve on the island, and remain a haven for dragonflies, butterflies and red squirrels as well as birds, including lapwings and warblers. With its attractive and tranquil wide harbour dotted with colourful boats and popular with visiting yachts, Bembridge remains an affluent resort village. A notable feature is the lifeboat station, isolated on the end of the long jetty by the car park. Despite its simple and somewhat antique appearance, it was built only in 2011, at a cost of around £7 million. It's a vital part of the safety cover for the millions of sailors who pass through the Solent every year. On certain days you can enjoy a guided tour of this windswept boat-perch. The rocky coast on its southerly shore is subject to erosion, and suffered major collapses in recent years which have closed this part of the popular Isle of Wight Coastal Path. Some sections near Whitecliff Bay were rerouted in 2013, so look out for revised diversion signs as you go.

Culver monument and Bembridge Windmill

The walk takes you up to the high point of Culver Down. The monument on top of the hill is dedicated to Lord Yarborough, who founded the Royal Yacht Club, the first of its kind, in 1815. This was later renamed the Royal Yacht Squadron, and today it has its headquarters in Cowes. Algernon Swinburne, the Victorian poet who lived at Bonchurch, knew and loved Culver Down, often seeking inspiration here.

A modest mud-brown landmark, Bembridge Windmill is the last surviving windmill on the island, restored and cared for by the National Trust (open mid-March to October). When artist J M W Turner painted the mill in 1795, land to the west had yet to be drained, and the sea formed part of the same view. Today the windmill stands as a fascinating piece of industrial archaeology. It dates back to the early 1700s and, although it ceased grinding in 1913, when the last of the millers went off to fight in the war, you will find much of the original wooden machinery, including the sails, still intact. You can view various artefacts on three floors and savour the views from the top. There are nature trails outside during school holidays.

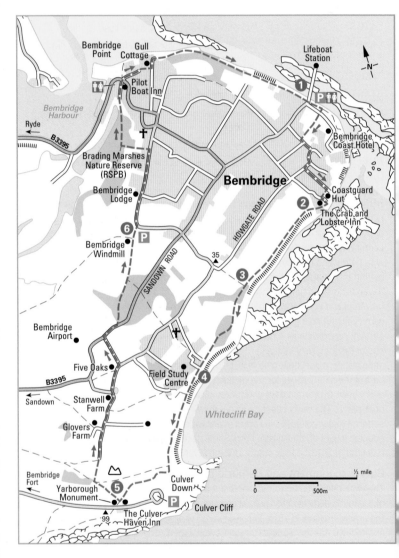

1. Walk to the sea wall overlooking the lifeboat pier, turn right and soon follow the coastal path inland. Cross the drive to the Bembridge Coast Hotel, and continue along the fenced path leading to a track. Turn left on the gravel track (Foreland Farm Lane) to a road, then turn right onto Howgate Road and take the second road (Beachfield Road) left. At the end, follow the coastal path right, pass behind the coastguard station and turn left in front of The Crab and Lobster Inn.

2. Walk across a small car park, passing steps down to the beach, go through a gate and continue ahead on the coastal path.

3. At a junction of paths turn left, staying on the coastal path, cross a footbridge and start to descend through the trees to a plank bridge. Rise up out of the woodland onto a level path passing behind the field studies centre.

4. Keep to the coastal path in front of Sandhills Holiday Park. Keep left across a green, passing a hut to enter an enclosed section of the path. Follow this past the holiday park and keep ahead as it rises then leads up steps to a stile. Follow the path steeply uphill to The Culver Haven pub.

5. Turn right at the monument and descend the field. Turn left onto the broad track. Cross a stile by a gate and go straight ahead, across a field to a second stile and gate. Follow the track ahead, which becomes a lane, passing Glovers Farm. At the road, keep right by a pond, and walk along the road with care. Turn left along a narrow lane just past Five Oaks. At the B3395, opposite Bembridge Airport, cross over and turn right down the gravel track. Descend and take the bridleway through the gate on your left, signed to Bembridge Windmill (BB36). Continue through Steyne Wood, then follow the track round right and uphill to the windmill.

6. Continue ahead and, at the road, bear left into Bembridge. After half a mile (800m), take the footpath left, signed to Bembridge Point, just after a large white house. Descend and bear right beside Brading Marshes Nature Reserve, to join a track to the B3395 at Bembridge Harbour. By the Pilot Boat Inn cross over into Pump Lane and follow it straight ahead (BB33), passing through a barrier to a lane. Go left, descend steps at the end to the beach, and walk along this to return to the car park.

Where to eat and drink

The Culver Haven Inn on Culver Down has the best views, and a seasonal kiosk nearby serves teas and snacks. The Pilot Boat Inn by Bembridge Harbour and The Crab and Lobster Inn on the clifftop serve fresh fish.

What to see

From the top of Culver Down you have magnificent views over the southeast corner of the island, across Bembridge Harbour towards the Spithead Forts and Portsmouth. To the west the view takes in the whole sweep of Sandown Bay and inland along the ridge of chalk downland.

While you're there

The derelict Bembridge Fort, west of the Yarborough Monument, dates from 1862, when the defence of Portsmouth against possible attack from France was deemed critical. It is being restored by the National Trust.

45 CARISBROOKE CASTLE

DISTANCE/TIME	6.5 miles (10.5km) / 2hrs 30min
ASCENT/GRADIENT	899ft (274m) / ▲ ▲
PATHS	Field and downland paths and tracks, some roads, 3 stiles
LANDSCAPE	Farmland and open chalk downland
SUGGESTED MAP	AA Walker's Map 16 Isle of Wight
START/FINISH	Grid reference: SZ489876
DOG FRIENDLINESS	Keep dogs under control
PARKING	Car park opposite Carisbrooke Priory entrance
PUBLIC TOILETS	There are toilets in Carisbrooke Castle, for which you will need to pay an entry fee or be an English Heritage member

On a spur of chalk downland, 150ft (46m) above the village, the site of a Roman fort, Carisbrook Castle, a grand medieval ruin, commands a perfect military location, overlooking the Bowcombe Valley and the approaches to the heart of the island. You can walk the battlements, experience the majestic location and admire the countryside below, much of the view encompassing the walk ahead.

The castle is probably of Saxon origin, but it was the Normans who strengthened the site, building the stone walls, the gatehouse and the keep, on a mound within the walls. The outer bastions were built to guard against the 16th-century threat of Spanish invasion. It was said that 'He who held Carisbrooke held the Isle of Wight.' For centuries the castle went hand-in-hand with the lordship of the island, before the Crown retained the lordship in the 16th century and appointed a 'Governor of the Island', a title that continues to be held today. The Great Hall, which was the official residence of the governor until 1944, now houses the Isle of Wight Museum. At the Carisbrooke Castle Story in the gatehouse, you'll learn more about the two occasions when it experienced military action, and find many exhibits about the castle's most famous royal visitor, King Charles I. He sought refuge here during the Civil War in November 1647, but was imprisoned by the governor until September 1648 before being taken to London for trial and execution. The king made two unsuccessful attempts to escape – you can see the window where he cut the bars before being thwarted. His children, the future Charles II, Henry, Duke of Gloucester, and 14-year-old Elizabeth (who died of pneumonia) were also detained here in 1650.

Leaving the castle, you'll walk through the Bowcombe Valley, beside the Lukely Brook, to the isolated village of Gatcombe, nestling in a valley. Quarries here provided stone for the building of Carisbrooke Castle. Each stone, it is said, was passed along a human chain to the site 2 miles (3.2km) away. Take a little time to explore the 13th-century church before joining the Shepherds Trail back to Carisbrooke.

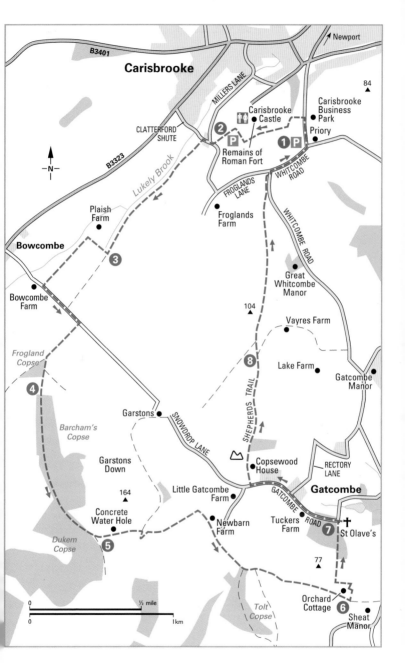

1. From the car park, and facing Carisbrooke Priory, turn left and walk along the road. Take the footpath (N193) left and go ahead past a gate, soon sloping through the trees. At the ruins of Carisbrooke Castle, bear left and follow the path along the castle walls. Turn left through a gate at the car park and follow the public footpath sign (N88) for Millers Lane, descending into a shady gully.

2. Turn right on reaching the road, pass the end of Millers Lane and walk to a kissing gate and path (N104) on the left, signposted 'Bowcombe'. Cross a plank bridge and turn left along the marshy field to a stile and cross the pastures. Cross two more stiles and keep ahead to meet a track, beyond Plaish Farm.

3. Turn right here and follow the enclosed path, bending left where the path splits after 150yds (137m). Turn left on reaching the track at Bowcombe Farm. Pass an unmarked footpath on the left, and soon turn right onto a track heading towards a belt of woodland. Veer left at the corner of Frogland Copse, signed 'Chillerton Down', and follow the field edge to a bridleway sign (N146 Gatcombe).

4. Bear right through the trees and continue ahead up the slope, skirting the field boundary. Go through a gate into the next field, enjoy the views east, then pass through the bridle gate and into the conifer-rich woodland of Dukem Copse. Follow the track inside the woodland edge as far as the signposted turning towards Gatcombe (G22) on your left.

5. Turn left through a gate and continue along the field edge. On reaching a path to Garstons, ignore the gate on the left but descend to the right and then swing left to a gate. Follow the bridleway down and turn right just before Newbarn Farm. Bear right at the entrance and, where the lane hooks left, keep right ahead along the bridleway (G6 to Chilerton). At the edge of Tolt Copse ignore the path right and bear left, soon to leave the Shepherds Trail, keeping ahead along a bridleway (G8 to Brook Lane) continuing towards Sheat Manor.

6. Before the manor, at a junction of paths, turn left, following the path past three cottages, then bear left again and keep to the winding path as it ascends to woodland. Proceed through the wood and descend to a lane beside St Olave's Church. Turn right to explore it.

7. On leaving the church, go straight ahead to walk along Gatcombe Road, pass Rectory Lane, then turn right on the bridleway (G6 to Gatcombe) at a driveway signed to Copsewood House, rejoining the Shepherds Trail. Pass between properties on a concrete track and then Copsewood House at the top. Ascend the narrow path and climb quite steeply through trees. Pass over a track, then go through a gate and follow the path round the left-hand field edge, the tall clock tower of Gatcombe Manor below and to your right.

8. Go through another gate and keep beside the field boundary. Rise up to another field and keep ahead on the public bridleway (N108 to Whitcombe Cross) and then into a shady gully which widens. Arrive at the junction of Froglands Lane and Whitcombe Road and turn left to reach the car park.

Where to eat and drink

Try the tearoom at Carisbrooke Castle (open April–October). There are also two pubs in Carisbrooke.

While you're there

Visit Carisbrooke Castle. Walk the battlements and savour the majestic view over the countryside, locate the two medieval wells, one with winding gear driven by a donkey, and visit the Carisbrooke Castle Museum.

YARMOUTH AND THE YAR VALLEY

DISTANCE/TIME	4.1 miles (6.7km) / 2hrs
ASCENT/GRADIENT	200ft (61m) / ▲
PATHS	Town streets, but mostly clear gravel paths
LANDSCAPE	Marshes, woodland and rolling farmland
SUGGESTED MAP	AA Walker's Map 16 Isle of Wight
START/FINISH	Grid reference: SZ353897
DOG FRIENDLINESS	Riverside trail great for dogs, but beware cyclists
PARKING	On mainland by ferry terminal in Lymington (pay-and-display); in Yarmouth town square or by harbour (pay-and-display)
PUBLIC TOILETS	In ferry terminal for travellers, otherwise none on route
NOTES	This island walk can be started from Lymington on the mainland

This walk up the Yar Estuary from the historic town of Yarmouth to Freshwater village is a delight, and can be done easily on a day-trip from the mainland. Lymington pier has a rail link and car park, and the Wightlink ferries leave every hour, taking just 40 minutes to cross the Solent. Yarmouth itself has interesting little shops, historic corners to explore and lots of places to eat. Arriving from the water gives you the best views of the solid, square castle, beside the ferry pier, built by Henry VIII to fend off the threat of a French invasion. Look out from the side of the ferry for the later date of 1609 scratched into one of the triangular stone piers on the wall, indicating modifications that took place at the start of the 17th century.

As you stroll around the attractive streets with their fishermen's cottages and splendid (if diminutive) municipal buildings, it's hard to believe that Yarmouth, essentially a medieval fishing port, was for centuries at the forefront of the wars with European neighbours. It was walled, and the natural inlets created by the river were rechanneled at one time to create a complete moat around the town but, despite its best defences, Yarmouth was sacked at least twice by French marauders, in 1377 and 1544.

Sir Robert Holmes

A key player in the town's fortunes was the flamboyant Robert Holmes, Irish-born sailor and buccaneer. You'll find his likeness in St James' church. Having overhauled a French ship on its way to deliver a marble self-portrait statue to Louis XIV, Holmes had the captive sculptor chisel his own face onto the ready-carved body. Holmes became Governor of the Isle of Wight in 1668, and profited hugely from piracy against the French and Dutch. He built a grand house (now The George Hotel), entertaining Charles II on several occasions, and remodelled the castle before his death in 1692.

The River Yar

Birdlife abounds on the expanse of saltings and mudflats of the Yar Estuary at low tide. As well as the common waders, look for the curlew and whimbrel probing the mudflats, the red legs of the redshank, and, in winter, the flocks of brent geese feeding in neighbouring fields.

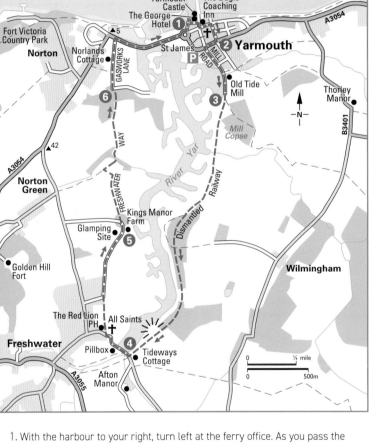

1. With the harbour to your right, turn left at the ferry office. As you pass the entrance to the castle on your left, it's worth a quick look down the alley even if you don't plan to visit (open April–October, dogs welcome). Pass Salty's Seafood Restaurant and the solid flank of The George Hotel to enter the square – actually three squares, named after the pier, the market and the church. Turn left to explore the wooden pier (toll payable), built in 1876 to accommodate tourists arriving by steamer and at 700ft (213m) one of the longest of its kind. Walk past The Bugle Coaching Inn, with the tiny redbrick town hall of 1763 on your right, to visit St James' church. Backtrack up the square and turn right down the High Street, then right again down South Street, passing charming Alma Place.

2. At the main road (Tennyson Road) turn right, cross over and continue towards the harbour. Turn left down Mill Road, and keep ahead on the gravel footpath (signed Y1) towards the old tide mill, built in 1793 to harness the tidal flow of the estuary. Cross a stile in front of the mill, ignoring the footpath left (Y2), and continue straight ahead.

3. Go through a gap by a bench and gate and turn right onto the former railway track, now a cycle path. Follow this for 1.5 miles (2.4km). The open marsh view, with Mill Copse to the left, and Kings Manor Farm on the opposite riverbank ahead, soon disappears as low oak woodland closes overhead, the trees laiden with honeysuckle, wild rose and ivy.

4. On reaching the old stone bridge of The Causeway by Tideways Cottage, turn right and follow the winding road, passing a pillbox, to All Saints church in Freshwater village. The church has various Tennyson family memorials, and a magnificent ancient brass of Adam de Compton set in the wall by the organ pipes. Take the waymarked path, signed 'Freshwater Way and F1', between The White Cottage and the churchyard wall. Go through a gate and along a gravel path. At a kissing gate, continue ahead up the tarmac road, passing the back of a row of bungalows and then a campsite with yurts on the left.

5. Turn left before the farm entrance, through a gate, and bear right along the edge of two fields to a gate leading into woodland. Emerge through a gate, cross over a drive and continue ahead up the gravel track, which leads between fields. Follow the track through a small wood and turn right up the field edge when leaving the wood. At the next gap in the hedge, with a gate on your right, turn left up the side of the field to a kissing gate to a path between field and wood. Go through a gate and descend into another woodland.

6. Meet a track (Gasworks Lane) and turn left, signed 'Freshwater Way and F1'. Follow this past Norlands Cottage to the A3054. Turn right and follow the pavement up over the bridge and past the busy harbour, back into Yarmouth. Turn left for the ferry terminal.

Where to eat and drink

There's lots of choice in Yarmouth, including local produce and freshly caught crab and lobster at Salty's Restaurant and Bar by the castle, and at The Bugle Coaching Inn on the square. The Red Lion at Freshwater offers good pub food.

What to see

Look out for the magnificent mosaic on the wall at the entrance to the castle. It portrays key moments and buildings in the town's history, with contributions from local artists. Sculptor Glyn Roberts' work can also be seen on the churchyard wall at All Saints church, Freshwater, illustrating a comic local tale. Smuggler Manny Young fell asleep in his boat, being drunk on brandy, and awoke to believe he had landed in France but he couldn't get over how similar it all was to the Island he had left behind.

TENNYSON'S FRESHWATER

DISTANCE/TIME	6.1 miles (9.8km) / 3hrs
ASCENT/GRADIENT	732ft (223m) / ▲
PATHS	Downland, field and woodland paths, some road walking and stretch of disused railway
LANDSCAPE	Downland, farmland, freshwater marsh and salt marsh
SUGGESTED MAP	AA Walker's Map 16 Isle of Wight
START/FINISH	Grid reference: SZ346857
DOG FRIENDLINESS	Let off lead on Tennyson Down unless signs state otherwise, and along old railway
PARKING	Pay-and-display car park at Freshwater Bay
PUBLIC TOILETS	Freshwater Bay

Away from the bustle of the resort towns, West Wight is a quieter, less populated area of great natural beauty, offering open countryside, rugged cliffs, wonderful views and fascinating wildlife. This exhilarating ramble encapsulates the contrasting landscapes of the area, from the wildlife-rich tidal estuary of the River Yar to magnificent chalk headlands and hills with their breathtaking views.

Solitary walks

Of the many literary greats who sought seclusion and inspiration on the island during the 19th century, it was the poet Alfred, Lord Tennyson, who chose to reside in West Wight. Tennyson and his wife Emily first came to Farringford House, a castellated late-Georgian house (now a hotel) in 1853. From the drawing room he could look out across Freshwater Bay and the slopes of Afton Down, a view he believed to be the most beautiful in England – 'Mediterranean in its richness and charm'. Almost daily he would take long solitary walks across the chalk downland, enjoying the bracing air, which he declared to be 'worth sixpence a pint'. The island inspired some of his greatest poems. 'The Charge of the Light Brigade' was written on the Down that now bears his name, and 'Maud', 'Enoch Arden' and the 'Idylls of the King' at Farringford.

Tennyson's poetry was so popular that he soon became one of the richest poets in the country. Combined with his magnetic genius and personality, he soon changed the face of West Wight, as tiny Freshwater became a cultural centre, attracting the most eminent Victorians of his age, including Charles Kingsley, Garibaldi, Lewis Carroll, Charles Darwin and Prince Albert. Farringford was the perfect place to entertain friends and celebrities, but it was time spent alone wandering the Downs or in the fine garden that made Farringford so special. They bought a house on the mainland and only returned to Farringford for the winter, when they were undisturbed. Memories of the great man and his family are dotted along this walk.

On Tennyson Down you will find the granite monument erected in his honour in 1897. On quieter days you can imagine the poet striding up the hill, dressed in his flowing Spanish cloak, wide-brimmed hat and stout holly stick, for his favourite downland walk. In Freshwater, step inside All Saints church to view the memorials to the family, while in the peaceful churchyard you will find Emily's grave and a lovely view across the serene estuary of the River Yar.

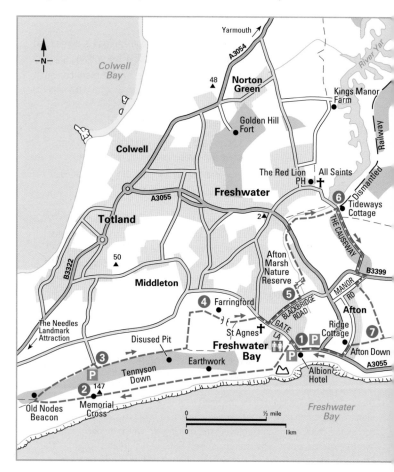

1. From the car park, turn right along the road, then left before the bus shelter along a metalled track, signed 'Coastal Path'. After 50yds (46m) bear right through a gate and follow the well-walked path, a gateway and up to the memorial cross at the summit of Tennyson Down.

2. Continue down the wide grassy swathe, veering right, which narrows between gorse bushes, to reach the replica of the Old Nodes Beacon. Here, turn sharp right down a chalk track. Continue through a gate and at a junction (with the car park on the right) keep straight on up the narrow path. At the top turn left onto grassy track.

3. The path widens then descends to a kissing gate into woodland. Proceed close to the woodland fringe before emerging into more open countryside. Passing a gate on the left, just beyond a disused pit on your right, turn left at a waymarker post down a narrower path. Go through a kissing gate, then follow the enclosed path to a kissing gate. Pass through and then walk along fenced path to a gate into a field and then another straight away out of the field.

4. Turn right and follow the path, passing a farm on your left, and then cross a gravel track and take the bridleway beside the wall of Farringford and pass beneath a wooden footbridge. Continue downhill to a gate and the road. (Turn left if you wish to visit Farringford). Turn right opposite the thatched church (St Agnes), and turn left down Blackbridge Road. After passing a pill box on your left and just a few paces before the bridge, turn left to enter Afton Marsh Nature Reserve.

5. Join the nature trail, following it across a footbridge and beside the stream to the A3055 (this can be very wet in winter). Turn left and almost immediately cross over to join the bridleway (F61) along the course of the old railway. In half a mile (800m) reach The Causeway.

6. Turn right, passing Tideways Cottage and follow this down to the B3399. Turn left and shortly after cross onto unmetalled Manor Road. In a few paces, bear left through a gate on a public right of way over private property, and ascend across grassland towards Afton Down.

7. Keep ahead at a junction of paths beside the golf course, soon to follow the gravel track right to the clubhouse. Pass in front of the building to reach the access track, keeping left to the A3055. Turn right downhill, on the pavement into Freshwater Bay and the car park.

Where to eat and drink

There are several cafés, pubs and restaurants in Freshwater, including the Albion Hotel, with its views over Freshwater Bay, and The Red Lion, which serves good pub food. Yarmouth also offers a choice of pubs, restaurants and cafés.

What to see

As you walk through the reedbeds and scrub of Afton Marsh Nature Reserve, look out for kingfishers and the yellow blooms of the marsh marigold, among many other birds and marsh plants that thrive there. On Tennyson Down you may see rare chalk-loving flowers and grasses, including bee orchids and nettle-leaved bellflowers, and hundred of small butterflies, such as common, chalkhill, small and Adonis blues, skippers and dark green fritillaries.

While you're there

Visit The Needles Landmark Attraction at Alum Bay. Take the spectacular chairlift to the beach to view the strange multicoloured sands for which it is famous, take a boat trip to view The Needles at close quarters, and explore the restored Old Battery, built in 1862, with its viewing platform and exhibition of the history of the headland.

DOWNLANDS TO BRIGHSTONE

DISTANCE/TIME	8.6 miles (13.8km) / 4hrs 15min
ASCENT/GRADIENT	1148ft (350m) / ▲ ▲
PATHS	Field and clifftop paths, woodland tracks, 2 stiles
LANDSCAPE	Farmland, chalk downland, woodland and coastal scenery
SUGGESTED MAP	AA Walker's Map 16 Isle of Wight
START/FINISH	Grid reference: SZ385835
DOG FRIENDLINESS	Off lead on Mottistone Down, otherwise keep under control
PARKING	Pay-and-display National Trust car park at Brook Chine
PUBLIC TOILETS	Brighstone

The heart of old Brighstone is one of the prettiest village scenes on the island, full of old-world charm with thatched goldenstone cottages, tea gardens and a fine Norman church. It is tucked under the downland ridge in the centre of the southwest coastal shelf, less than a mile (1.6km) from the coast, and the surrounding countryside is perfect for walking. In fact, the varied nature of the landscape here is a microcosm of the island as a whole. Stroll south through the fields and you are on the wild and beautiful shore, with miles of sand and rock ledges. Go north on to Brighstone Down, and you reach the largest area of forest on the island, dotted with Bronze Age and Neolithic burial mounds.

Smuggling history

A sense of history pervades Brighstone. At its tiny museum, you will discover its notorious past. From the 13th century to the late 1800s, Brighstone was a smuggling village, with many locals involved in wrecking and contraband. Good money could be earned salvaging cargoes and timbers from ships wrecked along the coast, and it was common for local children to seek credit from the Brighstone shopkeeper by promising 'Mother will pay next shipwreck'. It was not until the 1860s that the first lifeboats were launched from Brighstone and Brook. Reverend McCall aroused residents' consciences to Christian compassion for shipwrecked mariners, local benefactor Charles Seeley provided the finance and reformed smuggler James Buckett, having served five years' compulsory service in the navy as punishment for his crimes, became the first coxwain of the Brighstone lifeboat.

Three of Brighstone's rectors became bishops. Thomas Ken was rector in 1667 and wrote the hymn 'Glory to thee, my God this night' before becoming Bishop of Bath and Wells. Samuel Wilberforce was rector here for ten years, founding the library and school, before being appointed Bishop of Winchester. Finally, George Moberly later became Bishop of Salisbury.

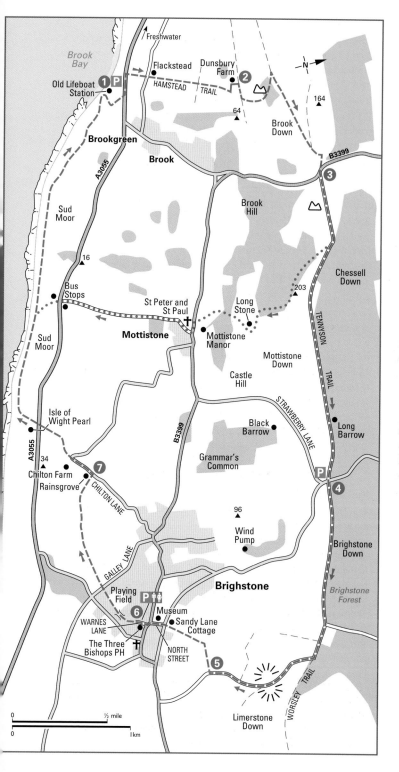

Brook Bay

Freshwater

Flackstead

Dunsbury Farm

HAMSTEAD TRAIL

Old Lifeboat Station

Brookgreen

Brook

A3055

Sud Moor

16

Bus Stops

St Peter and St Paul

Mottistone

Sud Moor

Isle of Wight Pearl

34

Chilton Farm

Rainsgrove

CHILTON LANE

GALLEY LANE

Playing Field

WARNES LANE

The Three Bishops PH

NORTH STREET

Museum

Sandy Lane Cottage

B3399

164

64

Brook Down

Brook Hill

203

Chessell Down

Long Stone

Mottistone Manor

Mottistone Down

Castle Hill

Black Barrow

Grammar's Common

96

Wind Pump

Brighstone

Limerstone Down

TENNYSON TRAIL

STRAWBERRY LANE

Long Barrow

Brighstone Down

Brighstone Forest

WORSLEY TRAIL

0   ½ mile
0   1km

167

1. From the car park, turn left along the A3055 to a stile on the right, way-marked 'Hamstead Trail', and walk across the field to a track. Keep ahead beside cottages and maintain this direction along a hedged path and then a field. On reaching a crossing of tracks continue heading uphill on a metalled track. Bear left then right around Dunsbury Farm to a T-junction.

2. Follow the road as it rises by the farmhouse to the brow and turn left up a track signed to 'Brook Down (BS49)'. At the junction of tracks turn right beneath telephone wires and pass through gate and onto Brook Down. Go through a gate and continue to climb, shortly bearing right onto a heavily rutted track to follow the track downhill beside a line of electricity poles. Keep right at a chalk track, go through a gate, to leave Brook Down, and cross the B3399 to a gate and bridleway, signed to 'Carisbrooke'.

3. Climb steadily along the main Tennyson Trail across the downland to a gate on the top of Mottistone Down. Just before the gate, pause and take in the view from the early Bronze Age barrows in the enclosures on the left of the track. Descend to the car park and turn right along the lane. After a few paces turn left along a stony track.

4. Follow the Tennyson Trail uphill beside Brighstone Forest. After passing a fork on the left, at the second junction of paths (opposite a fingerpost), take the bridleway right through a gate and descend Limerstone Down on a gorse-edged path with superb views. Ignore turnings left and right, and pass through a gate, ignoring the shady avenue of trees on the right. Then, just beyond a gate, turn right onto a grassy bridleway for Brighstone.

5. Head downhill through bracken and join a sandy path between trees to Brighstone. Cross the lane, walk down North Street, passing the village museum, to the B3399. Turn left, then right beside The Three Bishops pub into Warnes Lane.

6. Keep left of the car park, passing the school playing field, along a metalled path to a road. Turn right, then left with a waymarker and cross a footbridge. Keep to the left-hand edge of the playing field and to the rear of gardens to a lane. Cross straight over the lane and follow the fenced path to Chilton Lane.

7. Turn left, pass Chilton Farm and keep ahead at the sharp right-hand bend along a gravel track, passing holiday huts to the A3055. Pass through the car park opposite and follow the path to the coast. Turn right along the coast path, at the steps and soon cross a stile onto National Trust land (Sud Moor). Keep to the coast path, passing through three kissing gates to reach Brookgreen. Bear right beside the Chine and cottages, cross the bridge and turn left across the field to the car park.

Shortcut You can shorten this route by going via the Long Stone, and the church and National Trust tearooms at Mottistone. Having climbed steadily across downland from Point 3, go through the gate and after 60yds (55m) bear off right at the cross paths to follow the bridleway across rough heathland. Pass through a gate into woodland, and follow the path to a kissing gate. Turn left and follow the track to the Long Stone. Continue past the Long Stone,and take the narrow path on the left into the trees and undergrowth. Cross a track at a kissing gate and continue through the woods to the road by Mottistone Manor. Bear left, pass the church, and take the byway right behind the church (Ridget Lane). Follow the hedged track downhill to a gate and the main road.

Cross the stile opposite and keep to the right-hand field edge to a stile. Turn right at a third stile and rejoin Walk 43 along the coast path, crossing four stiles back to Brookgreen. Bear right beside Brook Chine and cottages, then bear left to a stile and return to the car park.

Where to eat and drink

On or just off the walk are The Three Bishops pub and the Pearl Café in the Isle of Wight Pearl complex. Afternoon teas are available in Mottistone Gardens.

What to see

Mottistone Down is rich in wildlife. Look out for chalk-loving plants like rock roses, horseshoe vetch and the clustered bellflower that flourish here. There are 30 species of butterfly that feed on the flowers, including chalkhill blues and fritillaries.

While you're there

The Long Stone is a free-standing upright stone of local greensand beside which lies another large stone. They are the remains of a Stone Age burial chamber, or long barrow, located behind the stone. They were erected some 4,000 years ago and in Saxon times were used as a meeting place or 'moot', hence the origin of the name 'Mottistone'. At Mottistone, you can admire the mullioned windows and ancient stone walls of the Elizabethan manor (not open to the public), and in the 13th century church of St Peter and St Paul see a Jacobean pulpit and wood salvaged from the *Cedrine*, a ship wrecked on the beach in 1862, in the chancel roof.

GODSHILL TO APPULDURCOMBE

DISTANCE/TIME	4.6 miles (7.4km) / 2hrs
ASCENT/GRADIENT	784ft (239m) / ▲ ▲
PATHS	Downland, woodland paths, tracks, metalled drive, 6 stiles
LANDSCAPE	Farmland, woodland and open downland
SUGGESTED MAP	AA Walker's Map 16 Isle of Wight
START/FINISH	Grid reference: SZ530817
DOG FRIENDLINESS	Dogs must be kept on lead in places
PARKING	Godshill, opposite The Griffin
PUBLIC TOILETS	Godshill, opposite The Griffin

With its village street lined with pretty thatched cottages, flower-filled gardens, wishing wells, souvenir shops and tea gardens, Godshill is the island's tourist 'honey-pot'. It is best explored out of season, when the coaches and crowds have gone, and its period buildings and magnificent church can be better appreciated. Godshill is also located in the heart of an unspoilt landscape and perfect walking country, making it a useful starting point for several exhilarating downland rambles.

Family tie

The history of Godshill is closely tied to the Worsley family, builders of the Palladian-style mansion of Appuldurcombe in the neighbouring village of Wroxall. Several buildings in the village were built by owners of Appuldurcombe and their memorials can be seen in the church. Your walk quickly escapes Godshill and the throng of summer visitors, steadily climbing through woods and farmland to the top of Stenbury Down, where you can catch your breath and take in the far-reaching island views, from Tennyson Down in the west to Culver Cliff in the east. You quickly descend towards Wroxall to reach the magnificent ruins of Appuldurcombe House.

Cradled in a sheltered and secluded natural amphitheatre beneath high downland slopes, Appuldurcombe House began as a priory in 1100. It later became a convent and then the Leigh family home from 1498. The connection with the illustrious Worsleys began when the Leighs' daughter Anne married Sir James Worsley, the richest man in Wight, who obtained a new lease. Following the Dissolution of the Monasteries, the Worsleys gained outright possession of the property, pulled down the old Tudor house and built a fine mansion with a pillared front at the end of the 18th century. They employed 'Capability' Brown to landscape the surroundings of the house. It was the grandest house on the island until Queen Victoria built Osborne House. It was sold in 1854 and became a school, the home of Benedictine monks, and a base for troops during World War I. Already damaged and decaying, it was finally reduced to a ruined shell in 1943, courtesy of a stray German landmine.

What you see today has been achieved by English Heritage and its predecessors, which since 1952 have repaired and restored the dramatic shell of the building, finally re-roofing and replacing windows in the Great Hall, Drawing Room and Dining Parlour in 1986. Visitors can wander through the eerily empty rooms, admire the splendid east front and stroll through the ornamental gardens and 11 acres (4.5ha) of grounds.

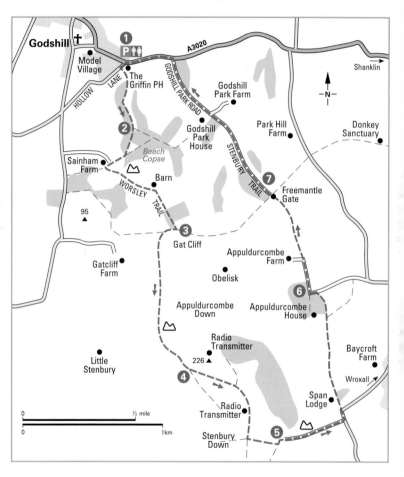

1. From the car park in Godshill, cross the road and walk down Hollow Lane beside The Griffin pub. Just before Godshill Cherry Orchard, take the footpath left, signed to Beech Copse. Keep to the right of the pub garden, pass through two kissing gates and continue gently uphill through the valley to a kissing gate on the edge of Beech Copse.

2. Just beyond, at a fork, bear right uphill through trees, on steps and board-walks, to a junction of paths by a gate. Turn right through the gate and walk towards Sainham Farm. Keep left of the farm to a gate and turn left uphill (Worsley Trail), signed to 'Stenbury Down'. Climbing over the stile, climb this fenced track, passing through two large metal gates to enter a copse.

3. Leave the woods via a stile next to large metal gate. At a junction of paths below Gat Cliff, take the bridleway GL49 right through a large metal gate beside a fingerpost, signed 'Stenbury Down'. Shortly, disregard the footpath right and keep to the bridleway ahead as it veers left and climbs to a gate. Skirting around the base of Gat Cliff and then Appuldurcombe Down, the path follows field-edges before climbing steeply through two gates beside a stone wall to a gate and open grassland on the top of Stenbury Down.

4. Keep left beside the hedge to a gate and then the same in the next field, in a few paces, bear right along the metalled track towards a radio transmitter. Pass to the left of the building then, just before reaching a kissing gate and footpath on the right, turn left through a waymarked gate on a fenced path between fields. Head downhill, then bear left through a gate to descend steps leading to a metalled track.

5. Turn left and steeply descend to a T-junction. Turn left, then, where the lane curves right, keep ahead, on GL47 to pass Span Lodge (formerly a gatehouse to Appuldurcombe House) and a large barn to a gate. Keep ahead between fields to a stile. Keep to the left-hand field edge in front of Appuldurcombe House, alongside iron railings and then a stone wall, to a stile by the entrance to the house.

6. Take the metalled road to the left of the car park, signed GL47 Freemantle Gate. Walk along the drive to Appuldurcombe Farm, then, where it curves left, keep straight ahead through two gateways (with stiles to the left) and soon pass through Freemantle Gate on the edge of Godshill Park.

7. Proceed downhill towards Godshill Park Farm. Ignore paths right and left, pass in front of Godshill Park House and join the metalled drive that leads to the A3020. Cross over and turn left along the pavement back to the car park.

Where to eat and drink

There's a good range of pubs, cafés and tearooms in Godshill, try The Taverners pub, the Willow Tree Tea Gardens or The Old World Tearooms and Gardens, all on the High Street.

What to see

Escape the crowds and the knick-knack shops in Godshill and make for All Saints church, a large, medieval parish church on a hill, surrounded by pretty thatched cottages. Look for the late 15th-century wall painting of Christ crucified (the Lily Cross), a painting which may be by Rubens, and the magnificent Tudor monuments to the Leigh and Worsley families.

While you're there

Visit the model village in the heart of Godshill, open daily, the buildings set among a fine display of shrubs and bushes. Part of the village shows Shanklin and Godshill as they were in the inter-war period. There is also a tearoom on the site. Appuldurcombe House, which is open six days a week, April–October (closed on Saturdays) is free to visit and passed on the walk.

BLACKGANG CHINE AND ST CATHERINE'S POINT

DISTANCE/TIME	5.4 miles (8.7km) / 2hrs 30min
ASCENT/GRADIENT	1142ft (348m) / ▲ ▲
PATHS	Field paths, downland tracks, coast path, 8 stiles
LANDSCAPE	Rolling downland and farmland, breezy cliff top
SUGGESTED MAP	AA Walker's Map 16 Isle of Wight
START/FINISH	Grid reference: SZ490767
DOG FRIENDLINESS	Keep dogs under control at all times
PARKING	Car park above Blackgang Chine
PUBLIC TOILETS	In Niton opposite the church

The viewpoint car park high above Blackgang Chine is the ideal starting point for this intriguing ramble around the island's most southerly point, an area steeped in tales about shipwrecks, smuggling and its three lighthouses. Before you lies the broad sweep of Chale Bay and high upon St Catherine's Hill to your right is a curious octagonal tower, known locally as the 'Pepperpot'. For centuries Chale Bay, in particular the treacherous rocks around Atherfield Ledge, was notorious for shipwrecks and the subsequent looting of desirable cargoes. Violent storms and huge seas drove fully rigged sailing ships crashing against the cliffs; once as many as 14 floundered in the 'Bay of Death' on a single night.

Your walk begins with a long, steady climb up St Catherine's Hill to the 'Pepperpot' and it is only here that you realise its significance. It's all that remains of a medieval lighthouse or beacon and is, equally, a monument to the folly of Walter de Godeton. Its story begins with the wreck of a merchant ship, the *Ship of the Blessed Mary*, at Atherfield Ledge in 1313, while bound for England with a consignment of wine. The sailors escaped and sold the 174 casks of wine to the islanders, one of whom was Walter de Godeton, who took 53 casks. As it belonged to a religious community in Normandy, it was considered an offence to receive the smuggled wine. Following a long trial, de Godeton was fined heavily and as an act of penance was ordered to build a pharos and oratory on the site of an earlier hermitage, so that a priest could tend the light and say prayers for those lost at sea.

The oratory has long since disappeared, but the lighthouse, operational until 1638, survives as Britain's only medieval lighthouse. Close by is another partially built lighthouse known as the 'Salt Pot'. Begun in 1785 to rekindle the St Catherine's light, the project was abandoned due to cost and the realisation that its warning light would rarely be visible due to fog. It was not until the tragic loss of the *Clarendon* in 1836 that the present lighthouse at St Catherine's Point was built. At the end of the St Catherine's Down stands Hoy's Monument, a 72ft (22m) high column commemorating the visit of a Russian tzar in 1814. The views from the ridge are spectacular and the walk culminates above the dramatic undercliff of St Catherine's Point.

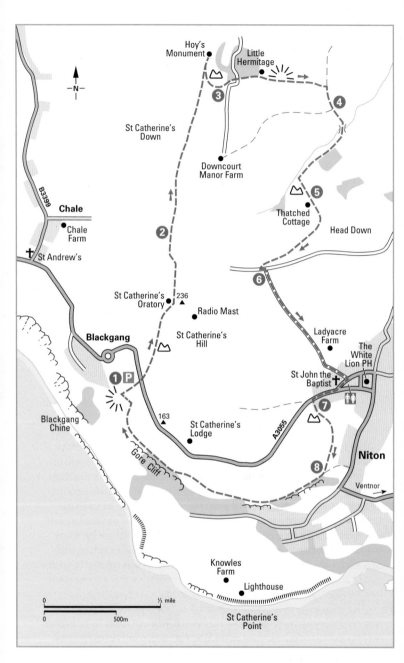

1. From the car park, cross the road and climb steps to a kissing gate. Bear left, signposted towards 'St Catherine's Oratory'. Steadily climb up the grassy downland to a kissing gate. Walk up to the old oratory, known locally as 'the Pepperpot'. Ignore the kissing gate by the trig point just beyond; keeping the fence on your right, continue downhill and bear left to a gate.

2. Go through the gate and proceed ahead on the broad grassy swathe to Hoy's Monument. Return for 80yds (73m) and take the bridleway left. Go through the gap and descend steeply through trees and bear left with the main path downhill to a gate. Follow the bridleway left, then at the stables directly ahead bear right along the driveway.

3. Proceed ahead at a crossing of tracks (Downcourt Manor Farm drive is to the right), heading downhill to a gate by a house (Little Hermitage). Walk alongside the right-hand field edge to a gate and head downhill on a hedged path. At a T-junction, turn right and go through a gate, the path soon emerging into a field.

4. Keep to the left-hand field edge, beside an overgrown gully, and cross the first stile on the left. Immediately bear right, then take the path ahead, with a gate to the right. Head through the trees, cross a concrete bridge and keep right. Gradually ascend a stony path, which can be very wet in winter, and which bears left to reach a stile, near a thatched cottage on your right.

5. Bear right through wide gap into a second field and turn left up the defined path rising up the slope to two stiles in the field corner. Cross the right-hand stile and immediately turn right, heading diagonally uphill across the face of Head Down to a stile. Turn left on a wide path, ignore stiles on either side and proceed to the one at the end of the track.

6. Turn left, then almost immediately right along a hedged bridleway. Head downhill, the path becoming metalled (Pan Lane) as it enters Niton. At the lane, turn right to enter the churchyard or left and then right for the White Lion. Leave via the lych gate and turn right alongside the A3055.

7. Take the footpath beside the last house (Tolverne) on the left and climb up steeply through trees to a stile. Walk ahead across grassland to a stile and follow the left-hand field edge to reach a kissing gate.

8. Turn right along the coastal path, through two kissing gates and emerge onto an open clifftop. Remain on this path near the cliff edge for nearly a mile (1.6km). Turn right onto a tarmac path for the final section to the car park.

Where to eat and drink
During the summer and at weekends you may find a refreshment van in the car park. The White Lion in Niton, once the haunt of smugglers, serves a varied menu and real ale.

What to see
The massive landslides around St Catherine's Point have created an undercliff world rich in wildlife. The tumbled land of hummocks and hollows with temporary ponds are the first landfall for migratory butterflies. It is also good place to watch migrating birds in spring.

While you're there
Visit St Andrew's church in Chale. It has withstood more than six centuries of storms, and from the churchyard, there is a fine view of this wild stretch of coast.

TITLES IN THE SERIES

- ▶ 50 Walks in Berkshire & Buckinghamshire
- ▶ 50 Walks in the Brecon Beacons & South Wales
- ▶ 50 Walks in Cornwall
- ▶ 50 Walks in the Cotswolds
- ▶ 50 Walks in Derbyshire
- ▶ 50 Walks in Devon
- ▶ 50 Walks in Dorset
- ▶ 50 Walks in Durham & Northumberland
- ▶ 50 Walks in Essex
- ▶ 50 Walks in Gloucestershire
- ▶ 50 Walks in Hampshire & the Isle of Wight
- ▶ 50 Walks in Herefordshire & Worcestershire
- ▶ 50 Walks in Hertfordshire
- ▶ 50 Walks in Kent
- ▶ 50 Walks in the Lake District
- ▶ 50 Walks in London
- ▶ 50 Walks in Norfolk
- ▶ 50 Walks in North Yorkshire
- ▶ 50 Walks in Oxfordshire
- ▶ 50 Walks in the Peak District
- ▶ 50 Walks in Shropshire
- ▶ 50 Walks in Snowdonia & North Wales
- ▶ 50 Walks in Somerset
- ▶ 50 Walks in Staffordshire
- ▶ 50 Walks in Suffolk
- ▶ 50 Walks in Surrey
- ▶ 50 Walks in Sussex & South Downs
- ▶ 50 Walks in Warwickshire & West Midlands
- ▶ 50 Walks in West Yorkshire
- ▶ 50 Walks in Wiltshire
- ▶ 50 Walks in the Yorkshire Dales